Yucatan for Travelers – Side Trips Valladolid to Tulum

By John M. Grimsrud
Edited by Jane A. Grimsrud

Dedication

This book is dedicated to John L. Stephens, Lilo Linke, Michel Peissel, Ronald Wright, and Michael Coe. These explorers and travelers wrote about their adventures in Yucatan. They inspired us to seek out the wonders of this magical land.

Contents

Introduction

Yucatan for Travelers – Side Trips: Valladolid to Tulum looks beyond the obvious popular tourist attractions, the luxury coast resorts, and the modern conveniences of big cities to discover the unique Yucatan.

From the Puuc hills to the extensive coast of Yucatan there are thousands of kilometers of paved quiet roads through countless Mayan villages interspersed with colonial haciendas and ancient Mayan ruins, all there just waiting for your visit.

This is photo-op and bird watching country that is the very finest this planet has to offer.

More than a quarter of a century of inspired exploration and recording of our travels while living in Yucatan has led to an impressive collection of outings that are the foundation for this book, built one story at a time.

We present the best of the best.

Over the years we have thoroughly enjoyed visiting Valladolid, first by narrow gauge train, (it no longer exists) and these days driving, busing, and cycling this unique end of the world with its year round tropical weather. We now have many adventures to share with you.

Get off the main roads and away from the trendy tourist attractions to discover the hidden places (gems) of the real Yucatan.

This book contains our favorite travel adventure trips of the places, excursions and outings, which we like for different reasons. Among them; tranquility, history, a view of quaint villages, a connection with the ancient Maya, changing scenery, and a look at another aspect of life that will take you out of the mainstream and off the beaten path.

This isn't just a guide book but an idea book. It is something of another element to give you direction with your guide books like Lonely Planet or Moon Guide.

The book is not made to compete with guidebooks—it is made to complement them.

It is essential that you get a copy of the Yucatan Today magazine for their good maps and helpful travel tips. It is free and available at most restaurants, hotels, and the information center on the central plaza in Valladolid.

Many of our excursions have been by bicycle and bus. Bicycle and bus excursions in Yucatan are by far the most inexpensive you will ever take and can be the most rewarding in not only health benefits but also in memorable experiences.

In a small village some young Mayan girls ran after our bicycles and stopped us. They said that they were learning English in school and wanted to practice. One girl said; "I am sure that you find our country strange and interesting, and if I went to your country I am sure that I would find it strange and interesting too."

For the armchair traveler and for people that have been to Yucatan before and think that they have done everything, *Yucatan for Travelers – Side Trips: Valladolid to Tulum* will open the door to another side of life not presented in tours or guided excursions. So, we invite you to step into this different dimension and build your memories in the manner the Mayas built their pyramids, one piece at a time.

John M. Grimsrud

1 - *Valladolid, Yucatan - Why Start Here?*

Steeped in history, Valladolid has enormous potential to entertain the traveler with a long list of historical sites and numerous fascinating side trips. You will want to home base here for several days to get a glimpse of this alluring one-of-a-kind place.

At the crossroads of Yucatan, midway between Cancun, Mérida, and Tulum, and with frequent bus service, the location of Valladolid is as good as it gets.

The old Spanish colonial city of 45,868 inhabitants (2010 census) still moves at a pleasant pace. It has numerous accommodations ranging from upscale to bohemian and dining options from authentic Mayan to Mexican, plus Chinese and Italian.

This is a bicycler's paradise with numerous delightful side trips that have the wonderful option of loading your bike on a bus or *colectivo* taxi in order to maximize your touring pleasure.

Valladolid municipal market.

One of the highlights of our frequent visits to Valladolid is the colorful municipal market, corner of Calle 32 and 37, which covers an entire city block. It shouldn't be missed.

Amazingly the official Valladolid tourist map completely overlooks it. It is located four blocks east of the central plaza down the hill from Cenote Zaci. The main attractions at the market are the typical Mayan foods and products that are unique to the area...this is the real Mexico that is often overlooked by the casual traveler.

The Valladolid municipal market in the early morning.

Some of Yucatan's finest delights are only available at such places as the market in Valladolid. Until you have partaken of these local favorites you haven't sampled the real Yucatan.

Homemade and homegrown items are sold by Mayan women who set up provisional shops daily along the sidewalks or at the market. One of the many items that can be found are white crackers that are three to a bag and unique to the Americas. They are made from yucca root, also known as cassava root, the root that tapioca is made from. They are very labor intensive to make, and these lightly sugared delicate treats must be sampled. Another delicious item found at the market is the fresh corn bread made of new corn. They are about six inches in diameter, a quarter of an inch thick and baked to a deep golden brown on a *comal*.

This lady at the Valladolid market is selling a variety of items. Her specialty is the fresh cornbread made of new corn.

The sellers' of bean filled *polkanes*, either fried or in the style of *píib*, guarantee you can't eat just one.

The tacos and sandwiches made of Yucatan's favorite, *cochinita pibil*, are also hard to resist.

Photo: Selling *polkanes*.

A tamale for breakfast? It is the favorite food in the Valladolid municipal market.

Tamales are a popular food throughout Mexico and are prepared in nearly a thousand different styles. At the Valladolid market a variety of fillings are offered in the *tamales*: chicken, pork, *xpélon* (a type of bean) *chaya* and egg, and ground beef. Each vendor has a specialty. Some feature steamed *tamales*, and others prepare their *tamales* in the Mayan style of *píib* (baked in a pit in the earth). Savory *salsas* that you add at your own discretion heighten the eating experience.

Many of the memorable events of travel are found in good food. On our fact finding journeys we prize above almost everything else these splendid local delicacies. In Valladolid nearly everything edible makes your trip worthwhile.

Locally grown produce changes with the seasons.

Jane is ordering breakfast at Valladolid's food court.

The municipal food court next to the El Mesón del Marqués hotel and across from the *plaza grande* (main plaza) of Valladolid is another good and reasonably priced place to sample distinctive foods of Mexico. The menus are mixed with Mayan foods of Yucatan and Mexican foods from other parts of the country.

Huevos rancheros make for a sustaining breakfast that will keep your bicycle in motion until noon with no gasps. They are served with tortillas, a bowl of bean soup, fried bananas, and hot sauce made of chili *habanero*. Chili *habanero* is fiery hot and a favorite of the people of Yucatan.

John preparing to eat his order of *huevos rancheros*.

Two complete meals with fresh tropical fruit juice were less than fifty pesos or just over four dollars.

Would you believe that this and several other local specialties can be had at the municipal food court on the plaza where lunch and dinners are available all day at very affordable prices?

Early morning breakfast at either the main market or municipal food court gets us charged up for the next leg of our bike/bus excursion.

Colonial Valladolid

The original Valladolid was called Villa de Valle and founded by Francisco de Montejo, El Sobrino (the nephew) on May 28, 1543, and was located on a lagoon between present day Colonia Yucatán and El Cuyo.

The site proved to be so unhealthy that the Spanish colonials relocated to the Cupul Mayan ceremonial site of Zaci and there founded the present day Valladolid on March 24, 1545. They constructed their main plaza on what was the site of a lofty Mayan pyramid, which provided ample building material for the new Spanish city. Valladolid was the easternmost extremity of colonial Spain and became known as the "Sultaness of the East." The Mayan people and the land east of Valladolid were never conquered by the Spanish and remained in the hands of the Maya until recent times.

Valladolid was just awarded the designation of *pueblo mágico* by Mexico's department of tourism.

While in Valladolid, don't miss a visit to the colonial styled municipal building which is resplendent with a collection of inspiring murals that are worth the trip to Valladolid just to see. One of the most impressive depicts a visionary Mayan shaman resolutely facing his impending doom.

The Caste War

Valladolid became a battle ground and the front line of the protracted Caste War (la *guerra de las castas*) that erupted here in 1847 between the indigenous Maya, the original owners, and the Spanish settlers of Yucatan. This war became the longest lasting insurgency in the history of the Americas.

The spark that ignited the bloody and prolonged Caste War was the execution of Manuel Antonio Ay in Valladolid in 1847. At that time Valladolid was an all-white city with no Indians allowed within its gates. See Chichimilá in Chapter 2, Cobá to Valladolid for more about Manuel Antonio Ay.

In 1901 the Mexican federal troops, under President Porfirio Diaz, came in with high-powered weaponry and drove the indigenous Maya out of their capital city of Chan Santa Cruz, (Chan Santa Cruz was renamed Felipe Carrillo Puerto). All Mayan men that could be rounded up were shipped off to Cuba as slaves. The Maya continued to fight a guerrilla war that drove the federal troops to capitulation and out of their territory by 1915.

Bloody skirmishes continued well into the 1930s. Germ warfare was used against the Maya who held out until statehood for Quintana Roo was achieved in 1974.

Valladolid has a small city museum, San Roque, in a former convent building on the corner of Calle 38 and 41. It seems to be down-playing the Caste War and Mayan involvement in Yucatan.

The Mayan perspective of the Caste War is represented at the Caste War Museum south of Valladolid at Tihosuco. See Chapter 3.

Zaci

Zaci was a principal Cupul Mayan ceremonial center upon which the present day Valladolid is built. Still remaining is the huge *cenote* of the same name. At Zaci you can dine at a restaurant overlooking that intriguing cenote. Interesting Mayan artifacts are displayed at the *cenote* museum.

This *cenote* is located on Calle 36 between Calle 37 and Calle 39, two blocks east of the central plaza and on the way to the municipal market.

Side streets of Valladolid

Side streets of Valladolid are quiet and interesting for bicycle excursions. You can rent a bicycle or bring your own.

We always travel with our folding bicycles, which easily stow in the luggage compartment of the bus, or inside or on the roof of a *colectivo* taxi.

If your time in Valladolid is limited, bike to the municipal market or one or more of Valladolid's five distinct neighborhoods, each with a historic church.

If you have half a day, consider biking to one or more of the nearby *cenotes*, villages, or to Ek Balam. MexiGo tours is the place to rent a bike and do your own tour, or take one of their guided bicycle excursions. They also have excellent guided tours that visit points of interest at a sensible rate and in the comfort of an air conditioned van.

Toon, his wife Vivyana, and their guides have a wide range of language skills and are very well-informed on what to do and see in Valladolid and the area. MexiGo Tours (www.mexigotours.com) is located on Calle 43 No. 204-C, between Calle 40 and Calle 42, directly behind the big downtown church.

MexiGo Tours are the ones to ask about where to eat and accommodations...I assure you they will make certain you get the very best quality, location, and at prices you will like.

Special Treats in Valladolid

Longaniza de Valladolid, greased to kill spicy sausage, but irresistible and worth the risk.

Sosa Xtabentun is a sweet honey based liquor that originated here. *Xtabentun* can be purchased at Compañía Sosa located on Calle 42, No. 215, between Calle 47 and 49 in downtown Valladolid.

Bizcochos, small bread sticks found in the bakery on the corner of Calle 39 and Calle 46 near the ADO bus terminal...knock-offs have become popular and are found all around Yucatan.

Tour guide books extensively describe Valladolid points of interest and the numerous hotels available. Our interest is showing you the other face of Yucatan; places away from tour buses and trinket shops, places that make you want to linger.

Getting there: See Chapter 19: Buses and Colectivo Taxis.

2 - Cobá to Valladolid – The Perfect Bike Trip

The wind and sun were on our backs, and the temperature was a cool 14.8° C. This incredible trip from Cobá through Chan Chen 1, Xuilub, Xocén, and Chichimilá to Valladolid is part of the story that follows:

Our trip started with a bus ride to Valladolid, and then a day of exploration to places near this tranquil colonial city.

Valladolid side trip to Tixhualactún

This sign greets you at the entrance to the little slice of nowhere known as Tixhualactún, "the town tourists miss most."

Tixhualactún is off the beaten path and is almost a suburb of Valladolid. It is in no way tourist oriented, but it has the unique feature of having been totally overlooked and bypassed. It is an easy and short bicycle ride south of Valladolid.

The most striking feature when you enter Tixhualactún is the huge crumbling old church, *La Iglesia del Santo Cristo de la Exaltación*, which is situated on the quiet as a ghost town central plaza.

In a state of nearly total neglect for the past three hundred years, the stacked stone structure has lost its massive roof to a cave-in, and the walls are in the process of taking departure in different directions; heading from the vertical to horizontal.

Outwardly you could easily assume that this decaying structure was totally abandoned, not so, it is actually still functional to a degree.

The information sign states that the church is three hundred years old and asks you to conserve its splendor and not take away any of the building's stones.

An interesting thought to contemplate here is the reality that the Spanish conquistadors were actually recyclers. All of the building materials used to build this old church and the entire community, for that matter, were in fact recycled from previous Mayan temples standing here.

Peering into the church you are in for several surprises. First, the most striking feature of all is that the entire roof has completely vanished, and the sky is the limit where a glimpse of heaven is afforded. The inner walls are devoid of paint and bleak with blotched mold interspersed with occasional outcroppings of vegetation. A tiny persistence of faith is evident here within the open air nave where a tin roofed pole shed protects the sanctuary's altar within the vacant walls of the church.

The walk of a few steps from the central plaza to this still ornately adorned entry door of the church is on a dirt path lined with knee high clingy weeds.

The Spanish conquistadors had overrun and expelled the Moors from Spain, but they took their trademark architectural designs to the Americas as can clearly be seen in the ogee arch and Moorish pillars of the church cloister.

The center of downtown Tixhualactún and the silent plaza and business district.

Even though the old church crumbled, and its bells fell to earth, they have been resurrected to call in the faithful.

The mystery is just what led the community that originally erected this monumental church to sink into three hundred years of apathy.

No tour buses or hordes of street vendors hawking their handcrafts to camera snapping sightseeing visitors will be found here, which in itself makes the little side trip worthwhile.

Wait! There is more to Tixhualactún. Adjacent to the main plaza is a *cenote*, in Maya *dzonot*. A *cenote* is a type of sinkhole that here in the limestone bedrock actually has flowing water. The water level in the *cenote* would be at the same level of area wells, which is the water table at about eighteen meters down.

We were treated to a strange display that continued all the time we were there. Huge flocks of bats were swarming, screeching, and circling nonstop at a hurried pace, around and around within the *cenote,* and we were lucky enough to capture this event on a video.

A little girl came on her bicycle to greet us in Tixhualactún. She was talkative, inquisitive, and full of town facts...a pleasant welcoming committee of one.

We bicycled back to Valladolid and arrived to see that the western sun was setting on the north facing cathedral that fronts on Valladolid's main plaza.

Valladolid's cathedral situated on the south side of the main plaza.

Our first stop in town was the municipal food court located across the plaza and next to the El Mesón del Marqués hotel.

John eating *salbutes*.

The traditional Mayan chicken *salbutes* are worth the trip, but be cautious with the lethally hot comatose level chili *habanero* sauce that could get you in the end.

After our first day of bicycling in the Valladolid area, Jane came up with a strategy for the next leg of this tour. We would bus to Cobá, bike the area, and visit the Mayan archeological site of Cobá.

The following day we planned an early start, and with the sun and Caribbean trade wind at our back, we would make our eighty-five kilometer return trip to Valladolid via a newly paved jungle road.

The archeological site of Cobá and the village of the same name are sixty kilometers from Valladolid on a direct route, and forty-four kilometers from Tulum on the Caribbean Sea.

Our home in Cobá is Hotelito Sac-be, our headquarters while biking the area and visiting the Mayan ruins at Cobá. Hotelito Sac-be is found on the main street just as you are entering the village.

There is a lagoon at Cobá that is filled with crocodiles. They have become semi-tamed by handouts that make them into a potential menace, especially with their large appetites and instinctive flesh fetish. The little girl in the above photo is tempting fate with her presence and could vanish in less than a blink of an eye. I have seen these seemingly slow reptiles strike with the speed of a coiled rattlesnake.

Midday at the Mayan archeological site of Cobá the crowd is nearly overwhelming. A feather bedecked bongo beating carnival side show that was definitely not Mayan had even materialized in the parking area.

Jane and I decided to wait until the crowd thinned and return when the shadows were long.

Afternoons in Yucatan are made for hammocks and siestas. Cobá is definitely a kinder, gentler place without heat stress and the masses. We find the slower we go, the more fun we have...this is a vacation after all.

Nohoch Mul pyramid at Cobá.

Cobá was one of the largest late-post classic Mayan temple cities. It has the tallest pyramid, *Nohoch Mul,* in all of Yucatan at 44 meters or 138 feet with 120 steps. Cobá was linked by a straight raised-paved *sacbe* road to their Caribbean seaport at Tulum and also Yaxuná, one hundred kilometers west. This huge temple is only restored on one side.

Returning to the Cobá ruins in the late afternoon, we made the rounds of the various temples by bicycle. Bike rentals and tricycles with driver/guides are available, but we preferred our own little folding bicycles. We were charged a small user fee for our bikes

Tricycle taxis await inquisitive temple climbers. This is a huge place that is best visited by bicycle or tricycle taxi. On foot, seeing the numerous temples would be too rushed to be pleasurable.

As the shadows become longer in late afternoon a serene ambiance floods over the jungle and the Mayan temples. Miraculously the crowd thins, peace returns, and the place

becomes enchantingly serene...you can actually feel the haunting Mayan magic.

The ghosts of the past seem to awaken as the sun slips over the horizon in the hushed twilight.

Early morning and late afternoon are preferred times to quietly visit the ruins.

Before six the next morning we roll west out of Cobá with a star studded sky, and the temperature is 14.8°C. Our day's jungle trek of eight-five kilometers is across a newly paved road. The area abounds in wildlife. There were so many parrots that we couldn't count them all.

On the road in the early morning.

The sun is up, but the air was still early morning fresh while we rolled into our first town of Chan Chén 1, a jungle outpost. Two hours of riding has gotten us here for breakfast in the little plaza.

At our next stop, Xuilub, the lovely silence was only punctuated by wild birds chirping and the occasional rooster. We loved the conspicuous lack of motorized vehicles and trash.

Xuilub is in the land of the pre-Hispanic Maya where all still speak the Mayan language, and they keep time honored traditions alive in cooking, farming, medicines, and dress.

This smiling lady is wearing the traditional *huipil* dress, and she carries on the time honored customs of the Mayan people in her village.

Roadside cross.

This green painted roadside wooden cross is a symbolic part of the Mayan Cult of the Holy Cross or Talking Cross. During the Caste War that began in 1847, which was the result of more than three centuries of oppressive servitude, the Yucatec Maya broke the chains that bound them. In an attempt to cling to their ancestral religion, they created a new version that incorporated their Mayan beliefs with Catholicism. Over the ensuing years a number of splinter groups have emerged. As you travel the back roads of Yucatan, be on the lookout for the little roadside chapels with their lighted candles and crosses.

Our next village on our route was Xocén.

Xocén, Yucatan, is home to the church La Iglesia *Santa Cruz Tún* (the church of the Holy Cross Tún).

La Iglesia de Santa Cruz Tún in Xocén.

The Mayan church of the Holy Cross is filled with symbolism dating back to pre-Hispanic times. We stumbled upon this sacred Mayan temple quite by accident.

The "Bienvenidos Visitantes" (welcome visitors) sign beckoned us to enter...and we did.

Warning signs are posted admonishing all who enter not to take any photos, and if you do, you will be punished by the municipal government of Xocén.

We were greeted at the entrance, and when I spoke Maya we were brought directly into an ongoing ceremony at the altar of the stone cross that until recently was forbidden to anyone not Mayan. There we were presented with a traditional and blessed bowl of *atole*. *Atole* is made of corn dough and honey. We were at a loss as what to do next, so we patiently watched to see what others did to get some clue. Meanwhile we observed the interior of the church.

The center of the low altar held the stone cross dressed in an embroidered vestment, and to one side were two smaller wooden crosses. Adjacent in boxes with glass doors were religious icons with a definite Catholic connection. A Virgin of Guadalupe was on one side and some saintly figures on the other. There was also a painting of Jesus Christ.

Before the altar was a long high table with a kneeling pad attached. The table top was covered with thirteen lighted candles. Thirteen is a sacred number to the Maya. Thirteen is the number of days in their week and the number of full moons in a solar year.

Next from a huge caldron we were given a bowl of *pavo en relleno negro*, a delicious dish made of turkey (turkeys are raised in the backyards of most rural Mayan homes) in a thick spicy sauce, along with handmade tortillas; all were blessed on the altar.

Now we had a bowl of food, but no eating utensils. Fortunately we had previously been introduced to the customary way of tearing a tortilla in two and rolling it into a cone to scoop out the thick sauce. The large pieces of turkey meat were placed, (with our fingers) in the tortillas to form tacos.

Next we were given a piece of sweet tortilla made of corn, honey, and chocolate, which was also blessed.

A Mayan man told us that this religious ceremony was held to ask God to bestow his blessing on a group of young people from a nearby village who were starting their long journey to the U.S.A. in search of work.

The same man also told us that he and the other farmers that were members of the Cult of the Santa Cruz Tún always held a similar ceremony every year to ask a blessing for good crops. He told us that last year he had an excellent crop, but his neighbor, a Catholic, had a dismal yield, thus proving the power of the Santa Cruz Tún. It is hard to argue with success!

Our next stop on our bike tour was at the Mayan village of Chichimilá, seven kilometers on a bike path short of our end destination of Valladolid.

Bicycling back to Valladolid, we spotted this green cross near Chichimilá, a town very important in the Caste War.

Chichimilá

At the center of town is a memorial to Chichimilá's native son and martyr, Manuel Antonio Ay (1817-1847). Manuel Antonio Ay was a leader along with Cecilio Chi and Jacinto Pat in the Mayan movement of liberation from oppression that was to become known as the Caste War, which began in 1847.

For Chichimilá, the Caste War didn't officially end until 1975 when a treaty was signed with the Mexican government.

Memorial to Manuel Antonio Ay in Chichimilá.

Manuel Antonio Ay was arrested, convicted in a fast trial, and on July 26, 1847, he was led out to face a firing squad. He was a small brown man, hatless and shoeless. His friends came to see him dic. The order was given to fire. Manuel slumped against a bullet-ridden wall in the patio of the Chapel of Santa Anna in Valladolid and became a martyr.

The white Yucatecans hoped that this execution would set an example for other rebellious Mayans and bring an end to rebellion, but instead it was the spark that ignited the long and deadly Caste War.

After coffee and a few tortillas for a snack, Jane and I, out of curiosity, wanted to check out the housing market, and two local men guided us to the only house in town for sale. It was just three blocks removed from the downtown business district, had a house with a palm thatched roof, city water, electric, and a well eighteen meters deep. This place was in the dense jungle with feral critters lurking nearby.

Our two Chichimilá guides and John at the entrance to the property. This slice of paradise required a lot of youthful exuberance to conquer.

Near to Chichimilá is the Cenote Xlakaj, which is operated by the people of Chichimilá. It is a beautiful cenote with easy access for swimming, cabins, and a restaurant.

We biked back to Valladolid and spent the night.

This completed three days of adventure in Yucatan.

3 - Caste War Route

The Caste War Route from Felipe Carrillo Puerto to Tihosuco and Valladolid.

"In the sixteenth century God had spoken to the Maya through Chilam Balam. In 1850, he spoke again, from a little wooden cross carved on a mahogany tree beside a cenote in the heart of Quintana Roo." Ronald Wright, Time Among the Maya, 1989

The story of the Cult of the Talking Cross (La Cruz Parlante) and the start of our journey along the route of Caste War sites begins in the seldom visited Mexican town of Felipe Carrillo Puerto, the former Chan Santa Cruz, Quintana Roo. This is where the Talking Cross prophesied victory to the Maya and told them they were the chosen race, the true Christians and the children of God. Although final victory never came, the Cross helped the Maya resist the Mexicans for fifty more years. Chan Santa Cruz was the capital of the Mayan territory during the Caste War that began in 1847. No Caucasians were safe here during the time of the conflict.

Chan Santa Cruz was overrun by Mexican federal troops in 1901, and the Chan Santa Cruz Maya retreated to the jungle to fight a guerrilla war that caused the federal troops to capitulate by 1915.

The Maya only returned to their old city of Chan Santa Cruz to fill poisoned wells and tear up the railway tracks connecting to the Caribbean Sea.

The Chan Santa Cruz Maya lived in relative peace and harmony with nature in their jungle territory. In 1936 some of the Mayan communities signed treaties with the Mexican government. At that time, the capital of the territory of Quintana Roo was relocated by President Cárdenas to its present location of Chetumal.

Today Felipe Carrillo Puerto is almost too peaceful and quiet. It remains the home of one faction of the Cult of the Talking

Cross, a relic of the Caste War and of the Mayan attempt to keep their brand of spirituality alive.

This beautiful Mayan lady is performing her rotating one week vigil at the Talking Cross chapel. The chapel is located on a quiet side street in Felipe Carrillo Puerto.

Former Mayan church of Balam Nah.

The Mayan church of Balam Nah where the religion of the Talking Cross was practiced was constructed during the Caste War. It is now a Catholic church.

Ironically, the large church in Chan Santa Cruz was built by slave labor. It was appropriately put up by captured Creoles (Mexicans of Spanish descent) under the Mayan whip during the Caste War. It has the distinction of being the last Mayan temple ever built.

The indigenous Maya had been enslaved from the mid-1500's under the Inquisition crazed Spanish. They had been forced to tear down their sacred temples and erect countless cathedrals and convents for the Spanish for more than three hundred oppressive years.

The Caste War had been a long time in coming and the Cult of the Talking Cross was a direct result of the Mayan attempt to regain their old religion.

The Mexican government recognized the Cult of the Talking Cross as a legitimate religion in 2002. Before that time the priests of the Cult were considered by Mexican civil law and the Roman Catholic Church as practicing witchcraft.

John in the *plaza grande* of Felipe Carrillo Puerto.

As I sat in the plaza nearby the former church of the Maya, Balam Nah, and with a statue of former Yucatan governor Felipe Carrillo Puerto behind me, I pondered the fate of the Maya and the events that happened here. I thought that these Maya missed a golden opportunity to erect a sacred pyramid to their gods of old.

The former governor of Yucatan, Felipe Carrillo Puerto, a Mexican of Spanish heritage, dedicated his life to rectifying many of the wrongs done to the Maya.

When the right-wing conservatives snatched power in Yucatan, the then governor Felipe Carrillo Puerto and his brothers were marched out to the Mérida cemetery and were executed by firing squad as they stood before their graves...that was 1924. With the popular governor dead, the Mayan hope for social justice died, and the Caste War continued to smolder among the Maya.

Felipe Carrillo Puerto doesn't have a lot to offer the tourist, but for the traveler and student of the Caste War of Yucatan it is a quiet place untouched by the hordes from the Maya Riviera and Costa Maya. It is a place where you can connect with and contemplate past events.

Time to move on: After eating some scrumptious *empanadas* for breakfast, we piled our folding bikes and gear along with about ten people into a *colectivo* taxi heading for Tihosuco, the next stop on our Caste War Route.

In the 1700's Spanish Tihosuco was a key outpost on the frontier. It was a prominent town with a huge church and many outstanding mansions.

We had just read Ronald Wright's account of his travels through Yucatan in his book *Time Among the Maya*, and we were anxious to visit the town of the Mayan revolutionary leader Jacinto Pat and to see the colossal sixteenth century church that was half open to the sky.

When Ronald Wright arrived at the church of Tihosuco, *"The priest was chasing a large pig out of the vestry. He was a Spaniard from Barcelona. 'The people here are better than in Spain,' he said. 'When Mayas get drunk they speak to God, when Spaniards drink, they deny him."* Ronald Wright, *Time Among the Maya*, 1989

We had our own encounter with a pig in Tihosuco, but not in the church.

The Tihosuco church is a bizarre relic of the Spanish Conquistadors. It collapsed in 1841 and was rebuilt, and then it was partially demolished by the Maya of Chan Santa Cruz in the Caste War. After that Tihosuco was abandoned for 80 years. To this day, the church remains in a state of frightful time-warp with its aged battle scars.

Looking out from the altar to the rear of this one-of-a-kind church, you are confronted by a shocking revelation. This otherwise complete structure has an entire wall missing, and it has been gone since the 1850s. If symbolic implications are intended, then this edifice conveys an almighty message.

At the time Ronald Wright visited Tihosuco, the church and the statue of Jacinto Pat were the only two points of interest, but recently the Mayan Caste War museum has opened. We were told by friends not to miss it.

We were in luck in that Carlos Chan Espinosa, the administrator, was there. Carlos is the man who makes this place work. He also aids the local community by bringing such valued services as food and lodging to visitors. Area homes are opened to travelers so that they can sample the home life of the region. This was positively splendid, and Carlos located a place for us.

The Mayan Caste War museum is on a side street across from the town plaza.

The Tihosuco museum has an extensive presentation on the Caste War and also a Mayan herb garden complete with many medicinal plants. Ongoing seminars and lectures plus numerous interactive community events keep the museum a vital part of the public information exchange.

Mayan ladies from Tepich visit the Tihosuco museum.

The traditional dress of the Mayan ladies of the region is a *huipil*. A scarf, known as a *rebozo*, is always worn also. The *rebozo* has a multitude of uses that include head cover, shawl, and baby sling.

The Tihosuco Caste War Museum depicts the Caste War from the Mayan point of view. The museum also has a collection of village artifacts that span centuries: clay figures, antiques, photographs, arrowheads, and pottery. All items were donated to the museum by the people of the town.

As part of the ongoing activities at the Tihosuco Caste War Museum, Antonia Poot, a museum guide, demonstrates the spinning of native cotton with talented coordination and her simple but authentic implements.

Twirling, with one hand, a tapered and polished shaft of *zapote* wood balanced in the base of a *jicara* bowl, Antonia deftly spins cotton from a ball with the other hand while miraculously transforming it into a neat finished product.

The cotton thread will, among other things, go into making candle wicks, which the local ladies sell along with a variety of herbal Mayan remedies, plus soaps and oils, in a shop fronting the main plaza of Tihosuco.

Jacinto Pat, a Mayan leader of prominence and large hacienda owner, was one of the driving forces that inspired the Mayan people to fight in what is known as the Caste War for their homeland, independence, and liberty.

Jacinto Pat is eternalized with a commemorative statue in the main plaza of Tihosuco.

Doña Lucia of Tihosuco and Jane.

Little Tihosuco has no restaurant, but you can get fed the exquisite local cuisine just by taking the advice of the museum administrator and visiting the home of Doña Lucia.

We weren't the only visitors that sought refuge with Doña Lucia. Doña Lucia had to turn away a wild javelina (wild pig) who wanted to enter.

A javelina in the doorway of Doña Lucia's living room.

As I was snapping photos of the javelina, Doña Lucia emphatically warned me of the aggressive savage temperament of these unsociable creatures.

Our cabin in Tihosuco.

By evening Carlos had us situated with Doña Agustina. This experience proved to be a highlight of our excursion.

The cabin was nestled into a heavily wooded lot just three blocks removed from the central plaza.

A spacious and clean bathroom adjoined our thatched roof cabin. Like something out of a storybook, our neat little cabin was a slice of paradise.

Here is the quiet Tihosuco street in front of our cabin looking north. You can see that this is ideal bicycle country.

We had the option of sleeping in a bed or hammocks. We naturally chose the hammocks because these were huge and custom made for the ultimate in easygoing relaxation.

In Doña Agustina's Mayan home there were a few innovations unavailable to her ancestors and many country dwellers to this day. Instead of cooking over an open fire, she had a gas stove, plus there were electric lights and water was available by turning on the tap.

Doña Agustina, our gracious hostess and wonderful cook, pictured above, quickly prepared a hardy meal suited to sustain active bicyclers...and it was delicious!

Early in the morning Doña Agustina is on her way to feed her chickens that were housed next to our cabin. Later she will go to the *molino* to have her corn ground into *masa* for tortillas. The magic of this corn was discovered more than three-thousand years ago here in Mexico when a process of boiling the corn in lime water the night before it was ready to grind (nixtamalization) not only

softened it but added the essential component that unleashes protein. This process gave a balanced diet to the ancestors of the Maya that led these pioneering people to the building of an advanced society.

The following morning, after our stay with Doña Agustina, we continued our bicycle tour on from Tihosuco to Tepich.

We paused at a roadside Mayan chapel. This is one of numerous roadside chapels where a spinoff of the Caste War Cult of the Talking Cross still worships in their special way.

A Mayan *huipil* embroidered dress adorns a wooden cross on the stone altar of the palm thatched chapel.

Tepich is our last stop on our Caste War tour before reaching Valladolid. Tepich has one claim to fame, and that is their home town hero, Cecilio Chí, who rallied his fellow Mayans in May of 1847 to rise up against the Mexican land owners in order to gain their freedom from oppression.

The inscription on his statue reads:

Glory to Cecilio Chí! Liberator of the Mayan nation and immortal symbol of justice and liberty.

This monument is in Tepich's small park and adjacent to the main highway.

The rustic church of Tepich is perched upon the remnants of a Mayan temple.

The church originally had a palm thatched roof but now has one of corrugated sheet metal.

Adjacent to the church is a forlorn graveyard where the town hero, Cecilio Chi, was buried in 1848.

The best thing to be said about no-frills little Tepich is that bus and *colectivo* taxi service are excellent, especially if you have a folding bicycle.

We ended our Caste War tour here and took a *colectivo* taxi north to Valladolid.

The Cult of the Talking Cross and the Caste War

The Caste War was a protracted battle between the Yucatec Maya and Mexican Spanish colonialists of Yucatan.

In early 1850 the insurgent Maya found themselves on the brink of defeat and sought refuge in the jungle of Quintana Roo where they established small communities. At this time, the Talking Cross appeared near a cenote in Chan Santa Cruz (present day Felipe Carrillo Puerto). The cross spoke to the Maya and promised them they would be safe from the bullets of the "whites" and ordered them to drive all the invaders from their land.

In time, a large church called the *Balam Nah* was built with captive white labor. The Talking Cross was then relocated there. The government troops took Chan Santa Cruz and destroyed the cross, but the Talking Cross gave birth to three sister crosses. These crosses are worshiped and guarded to this day.

One faction of the Cult of the Holy Cross is in Tulum, one remains in Felipe Carrillo Puerto, and another in Chompom. The government has recently constructed new chapels to house these crosses.

4 - Tihosuco – A Happy Ending

In 1686 the Dutch buccaneer Laurens de Graff came to Tihosuco and sacked it. Laurens was described as tall, blond, mustached, and handsome. In 2011 another handsome Dutchman arrived in Tihosuco, and he left Tihosuco with a beautiful bride and wonderful memories.

In 1544 Montejo the Younger of Spain captured the isolated Cochuah Mayan jungle town of Tihosuco. In the sixteenth century the Franciscans built the mighty fortress church in Tihosuco to defend their faith and their lives. By the mid-1700s, Tihosuco had a growing immigrant population and large haciendas flourished. Tihosuco was the last outpost of the Spanish colony and was surrounded by hostile Maya and subject to pirate attacks.

The great church of Tihosuco was ruined in the Caste War. Tihosuco first fell to the Mayas under the leadership of Cecilio Chi in the first days of the Caste War. The Yucatecans recovered the town in 1848. The Maya continued to attack the town, and in 1856 the citizens abandoned it to the jungle. When the populace came back 80 years later, it was the Maya who claimed the land.

The Dutch connection continues: This story amazingly unfolded because of a string of events that began in cyberspace. Ryan Barras, the Dutch connection, from Netherlands and Dominique, his Mexican fiancée, living in Miami, Florida, decided that they wanted to be married in Tulum, and they began looking for a suitable church. Ryan happened across a story on our website featuring Tihosuco, the Caste War, and the hauntingly unique church of Tihosuco.

Here, I will let Ryan tell you, in his own words, the rest of the story.

Ryan wrote: ...we just wanted to thank you for writing about the church. If it wasn't for your blog, I may have never found it, or heard about it. So, thank you again.

In any case, we decided to have our wedding near Tulum on 11-11-11, and I decided in February of this year to go visit the area to seek a hotel, reception location, and church for our ceremony. I had no idea what Catholic churches might be in the area, but when I started my research online, I came across your blog and more specifically, your description of the church of Tihosuco.

We were both taken aback by its beauty and the idea to have a wedding ceremony in a church that is part-ruin, or perhaps better said; a ruin that is a church.

Tihosuco church. Photo courtesy of Ryan Barras.

When I visited in February, I went to see the church, and my wife, who is Mexican, spoke to the priest (Father Angel) by phone and set up the appointment for me (my Spanish is very limited). Although when I met the Father, we didn't speak each other's languages, we communicated very well (of course, the tequila he kept offering me helped smooth things over as well!)...

It was a bit far from Tulum, and as you know, somewhat off the beaten path...so we were unsure we could do it to our guests to put them in a bus 2.5 hours to go to the church and back...but we decided to go ahead with it anyway. Our approximate 100 guests consisted of many of my best friends and family from Europe, many of our friends from around the United States, and many of my wife's friends and family from throughout Mexico, mostly Mexico City. The guest that traveled the furthest came from South Korea to be with us.

I am sure that this little town has never seen such a variety of guests from different cultures, and Father Angel was excited about the prospect of having an international wedding in his church! He also kept saying we were crazy! But let me tell you, when our guests laid eyes on the church, they were stunned, just breathless.

The Father was amazing, he treated us as family, he arranged for the local schoolchildren to partake and sing in our wedding – right alongside of our closest friends that happen to be a harpist and a jazz singer - they played and sang the Ave Maria for us in this magnificent church. He also searched for an English speaking priest from the area to preside over the ceremony so all would understand. His assistant arranged a red carpet, and flowers for the ceremony which were very sweetly arranged in white plastic buckets along the aisles...very touching! It was quite a sight to be seen!

Some of the local townspeople joined our ceremony, many others watched from a distance outside, and you could hear a few of them say 'there comes the artist!' when my wife appeared in her wedding dress (apparently, a few thought that this 'production' was a *telenovela*).

We also had a harp brought in from Cancún (for our friend to play on) from a local harpist that plays in Cancún's symphony orchestra...there are only 2 such harps in all of Mexico. The harpist was a bit baffled that we asked him to drive so far with his harp for our wedding, but when he saw the church he was also in awe and insisted that when he marries, it will be in this church as well. Many of my wife's friends from Cancún were also impressed by the church, never having known of its existence.

All in all, the day was labeled 'amazing', 'beautiful' and 'magical' by our friends and family...the tone of the group was also very nice and respectful, mindful of the conservative mindset of the area, and the privilege we were given to wed in their church.

Dominique and Ryan Barras. Photo courtesy of Ryan Barras.

Of course, we, and our guests, left the church a nice donation, and have asked Father Angel what else we can do for the people and the church...for my wife and I, we truly feel this is 'our church' as well now, and Father Angel made us promise to return to the church when we have our first child.

Ryan & Dominique Barras

For more about Tihosuco, see chapter 3.

5 - Church Route

Ruta de las Iglesias in the Jungle State of Quintana Roo

This is a fascinating route that explores the many churches built during the conquest of Yucatan, Caste War history, and Mayan villages of the present time.

The eastern part of what is now the State of Quintana Roo has the distinction of having remained in the hands of its original occupants, the indigenous Maya until recent times.

It has been speculated that a shipwrecked Spanish mercenary in the early 1500s named Gonzalo Guerrero, who married a Mayan princess, had the first *mestizo* children, and took up the Mayan ways, altered Yucatan history for the next four-hundred plus years. Gonzalo, a product of Inquisition crazed conquistadors who fought and won a seven hundred year war that drove the Moors and Jews out of the Iberian Peninsula, taught Spanish war tactics to his newly adopted Mayan countrymen.

The net result of all this is that many of the Mayan people of present day Quintana Roo have never lived under the oppressive *hacienda* system. Many of the Maya of today in Quintana Roo are independent, community minded, and self-sufficient, as a result of having fought the longest lasting insurgency war in the history of the Americas.

This route you are about to read about is situated on the front battle line of that war that still seethes in some villages to this day.

We used José Maria Morelos, Quintana Roo, also known as Kilometer 50, as a beginning point for this seldom traveled route. Valladolid was our end destination.

On the way to begin the *Ruta de las Iglesias,* (route of the churches) we passed first the town of Dziuché, with its one hotel. Dziuché is situated near the Laguna Chichancanab, a lake which is fifteen kilometers in length. The lake has public access with a swimming beach, pavilion, and dock.

Two kilometers down the road from Dziuché is a very bizarre local tourist attraction at Kantemó. The tourist brochure clearly stated about Kantemó: "You will encounter the spectacular cave of hundreds of hanging serpents clustered in the ceiling. The serpents snatch bats as the bats leave the cave every day."

This strange tourist attraction begins with a guided bicycle tour to the cave. The tour guide is equipped with an antivenin snake bite kit. Face masks are provided for all visitors to avoid respiratory diseases that may be contracted from bats. In addition to this tour, there is a foot path through the marsh with a wooden pier, a *cenote,* kayak rentals, and a bird observation tower that overlooks the lagoon.

MexiGo Tours in Valladolid offers guided tours to the serpent and bat caves.

This attraction is not for everybody.

Because of the distances and time constraints on this route, we hired a taxi to carry us to the furthest part of the *Ruta de las Iglesias* to begin our bike tour at the tiny isolated village of X-Querol near the Yucatan border.

We did not want to rush through this beautiful out of the tourist loop area without having enough time to thoroughly enjoy the many nearly forgotten little villages.

Our jovial taxi driver, Armando Sanchez Sandoval, entertained us with hilarious stories of his three wives and many *desechable,* "throw away" children.

At the end of the line in the village of X-Querol we unloaded our folding bicycles and packs from the taxi and began our visit to a strange world where we were the only tourists.

Our taxi driver Armando Sanchez Sandoval and Jane at X-Querol.

The road that ends in X-Querol is part of an ancient Mayan *sacbe* highway, which within a few meters becomes a footpath where it enters the dense jungle.

Last spring we attempted to bicycle across this same road but started from the Yucatan side in the tiny town of Ichmul. We wanted to visit a Mayan ruin that is along the *sacbe.*

We quickly discovered that it would even be a difficult trip by horse. Now we would take a different approach.

The main plaza in the quiet as a tomb village of X-Querol casts an eerie spell on this place that is nearly deserted and passed by time. Evidence of the ancient Mayan ceremonial center that once stood here is scattered in mounds throughout the town. The old *sacbe* road of the Maya still leads into the jungle towards the once important Mayan center of Ichmul. One can feel here this place is holding its breath waiting for its rebirth.

Traffic through the little outpost town of X-Querol with its eighty-five inhabitants is nearly nonexistent.

The rest of the world may self destruct, but here in X-Querol the residents will continue to feed themselves in the way they have since the day over four hundred years ago when the Spanish arrived to disrupt their lives.

Author Lilo Linke visited this remote jungle area in 1947, before the first roads into the area. Lilo said of these *milpa* farmers and their corn farming:

The zapote trees could be bled only during the rainy season. The rest of the year the men worked in their milpas. This was often an even harder task than the gathering of the chicle gum, an endless struggle against the jungle which stretched greedy arms towards the maize (corn). Every few years the men had to move on to new plots since the poor topsoil was soon exhausted. The bush was burnt down— which had the additional advantage of eliminating ticks and other vicious insects and a good many snakes—and then the slow labour of sowing started. For each seed a small hole was drilled into the soil with a short pointed stick, and the seed covered by pushing the earth over it with the feet in a dance-like movement. Then followed the anxious months of weeding and waiting: Birds had to be scared away, beetles and their grubs destroyed, the approaching armies of ants watched and diverted. Often the men had to carry water from miles away. And right to the end it was never certain whether there would be anything left to harvest. What triumph when the men at last could walk from plant to plant to break off the cobs and throw them into the baskets strapped to their shoulders! The stalks were left standing and burnt. And a few months after the whole weary process started all over again.

The same processes are still used today.

Farmers drying their corn in the old traditional way of the Maya.

Church of X-Querol.

We visited the forlorn church of X-Querol. This little church was never completed because of the bloody Caste War.

New house in X-Querol.

After a hurricane that devastated many homes in X-Querol, a government program for rural assistance brought new cement-block houses to X-Querol. They are very small, so additions are added; a kitchen cooking room and laundry utility area are neatly melded together.

Another government program furnished ecological cooking stoves to ten homes at a price equivalent to about $200 per stove. These stoves are designed to burn wood much more economically and also keep the smoke out of the cooking area in order to improve the women's health.

In traditional Mayan homes, the women cook over open fires, and many women suffer from life-threatening lung diseases because of the inhalation of wood smoke.

Nice roads with no traffic are a big draw and are hard to find in this day and time. The fresh air and wild jungle make our bicycle tour here well worth the effort especially when you consider that anywhere we are on this trip, if we decided to, we could be back home in Mérida before the sun went down.

On the road to Sacalaca.

After X-Querol, we head south along the quiet jungle road to our next town of Sacalaca.

The Mayan meaning of the name Sacalaca is the place of white grass and refers to the tall grass with broad leaves that grows abundantly here.

On road signs and maps "z" and "s" are often interchanged thus the road sign reads: Zacalaca. Every day in México is an adventure!

Santa Maria church at Sacalaca.

Time, Mother Nature, and the forces of gravity are relentlessly returning the church in Sacalaca to ground level. The 18th century Santa María Sacalaca church is awaiting restoration and has several stone statues in storage until renovation is completed.

The only congregation we found here was a gathering of the village drunks assembled under a tree in the front yard of this roofless dwelling, a relic of pre-Caste War times.

This chapel on the outskirts of town serves as the parish church.

The little town of Sacalaca quietly waits for something to happen.

With two old churches, a museum, and *cenote,* it would seem that curious visitors would be packing the streets, but it is so quiet and still that it appears to be totally forgotten.

Mounds from ancient Mayan ruins are scattered throughout the area.

This is just the kind of place that we dream of finding for one of our bicycle/bus/taxi excursion adventures.

On the main street of Sacalaca, houses of sticks, stones, and palm thatch are the standard. All of the building materials come from the local environment.

Notice the tall trees here in Quintana Roo. The blessing of ample rain and soil allow for prosperous agriculture

Heading north on the *Ruta de las Iglesias* to Sabán.

Heading to our next destination of Sabán, we noticed a conspicuous lack of motor vehicles. Except for the chirping birds it is so quiet here you can hear a car coming from many kilometers away.

Sabán church.

When you see a church the size of the one in Sabán you know that there had to be a sizable Mayan temple nearby to mine for building materials.

The baroque style columns and other ornate adornments of the massively built church of San Pedro is a classic example of 18th century Yucatecan frontier architecture.

During the Caste War these symbols of Spanish imperialism were not maintained. As a net consequence many of the roofs came crashing down and have never been rebuilt.

When the church structure was erected in 1795, Sabán had a Spanish population of 2,259 and was only second in size in this area to nearby Tihosuco.

During the Caste War the church and fine homes of the Spanish colonials were abandoned and Sabán remained a ghost town as late as 1950. Slowly new settlers moved in and retook the jungle.

A lovely park in front of the old church appears idyllic, but across the plaza the small shops in a market area were emitting an ear splitting racket with megaphones turned up to overdrive. This was not music but obnoxious noise. Other than this noise we found Sabán quaint, friendly, and interesting. It is definitely isolated and totally off of any tourist routes.

These smiling children of Sabán tagged along with us throughout the town.

Continuing on the *Ruta de las Iglesias,* our next stop was at nearby sister city Huaymax. The barefoot children ran along with us. As our bicycles raised a cloud of dust, their number continued to increase just like we were the Pied Piper.

Church at Huaymax.

Another victim of the Caste War; the church at Huaymax still has remnants of its charred ceiling beams in the choir loft.

The roofless building had been left to Mother Nature and time until recently when some of the villagers cleaned it up and began worshiping there on the same site as their converted ancient Mayan ancestors had done centuries previously.

View of interior of roofless church.

Plaster, paint, and a bell, among other things, brought the old war torn structure back from its 1848 snooze.

After over 160 years of neglect the place is back in business and it looks like the sky is still the limit with no roof to get in the way.

Resurrected from the dead with paint, adornments, and electric lights, this center of worship in Huaymax lives again.

After our tour of Huaymax we headed north towards Tihosuco. We encountered an obstacle and that was a road totally torn up with rebuilding in progress. We luckily found a taxi. We got the driver out of his hammock, interrupting his afternoon siesta, and we loaded our folded bicycles in his trunk.

We hadn't gone but a couple of kilometers and the sky opened up with a torrential tropical downpour. We felt fortunate to be in the taxi.

As we rolled into Tihosuco the weather cooperated like magic and the rain ceased.

Tihosuco is the most historic and interesting of the towns in the *Ruta de Las Iglesias*.

For an in-depth look at Tihosuco and its historical significance that led to the Caste War, see chapter 3: The Caste War Route and chapter 4: Tihosuco - A Happy Ending. There you will visit the old war ravaged church, the museum, and some of the interesting people that make Tihosuco their home.

Elly Smeenk with Tihosuco guests at the wedding of her son Ryan Barras on November 11, 2011, at the unique church at Tihosuco. Photo courtesy of Ryan Barras.

From Tihosuco, we bicycled on to Tepich, our last stop on the *Ruta de Iglesias* of Quintana Roo, before our end destination of Valladolid in Yucatan. Tepich is covered in chapter 3: The Caste War Route.

Tepich has been carved out of the encroaching jungle and lies on the border with Yucatan and Quintana Roo. The contrast between the two states is striking. Yucatan is semiarid and has a low scrub landscape where farming is marginal. Quintana Roo, by contrast, benefits by its proximity to the warm Caribbean Sea that regularly sends welcome rain to keep it green and lush.

Useful Information:

Kantemó serpent and bat tours

MexiGo Tours of Valladolid: www.mexigotours.com

Information of the bat caves of Kantemó:

http://www.cdi.gob.mx/ecoturismo/quintanaroo_kantemo. html

Related Chapters:

Chapter 3 - The Caste War Route

Chapter 4 - Tihosuco - A Happy Ending

6 - Peto and Ichmul

Peto is not the average tourist's end destination.

Only a few decades ago Peto was the end of the line for modern civilization and the rail line. It was on the frontier where the jungle began.

Mérida, 1985, – Jane boards the packed to capacity narrow gauge train to Peto with its 1890s vintage wooden coaches that were still rolling in 1985. The toilet was a hole in the floor.

Twenty-five years ago Jane and I departed Mérida on the narrow gauge train for one of our most memorable Yucatan adventures...we still have the original timetables and tickets.

We set off from Mérida aboard one of the last narrow gauge trains still operating in the world and headed into an unknown realm at the end of the line.

Back then Peto enjoyed a thriving export economy based on honey and *chicle*. *Chicle* is used in chewing gum. It was extracted from the sap of the towering zapote tree forest surrounding this area.

Riding aboard that long forgotten relic of the past that made six scheduled stops where there was only a foot path from the countryside, the conductor told us that he had been working onboard this train for twenty-six years, and we were the first foreigners to ride it all the way to the end of the line at Peto.

At Peto the entire train pulled to a stop for the night in the serene city center blocking intersections. The train would depart Peto at 5 a.m. the next morning and backup all the way to Mérida.

Read more about the history of transportation in Yucatan in chapter 18: Yucatan Roadways.

We were in another world so quiet it made you want to whisper. This sleepy colonial hamlet was dimly lit by sparse incandescent street lamps while the faint aroma of spicy wood smoke from neighborhood cooking fires trailed through the jungle scented evening air.

We dispersed on foot with the rest of our fellow passengers into the eerie dimness of Peto's silent night unhindered by traffic save the occasional bicycle.

Infrequently a dog would bark or a distant car started that could be heard putt-putt-putting slowly along and then silence returned. Tranquility was at its optimum here.

The first of the two hotels in town was fully booked, and the second had but one room remaining...we took it. The night clerk proudly signed me in as Mr. John and went out to get us a bar of soap, something normally not included in the accommodations inventory.

My first impression of our startlingly stark room was that it must have been of pre-Mayan origins. The stacked stone structure was in the evolutionary process of returning to the earth from which it had undoubtedly originated untold years beforehand. It appeared to be leaning in six directions at the same time, if that is at all possible.

In the corner of our primeval room stood a small battered gray baked enamel wash basin on an ornate antique metal stand undoubtedly forged by a blacksmith eons before. A single pipe dangled down from the ceiling with a garden spigot valve to fill the washbasin...there was no drain. We deduced that in order to dispose of the wash water, you merely pitched it out the barn door sized window that had no glass or screen; the birds were free to flutter in and out.

Some discretion in pitching waste water out the window was in order because of a makeshift movie theater set up next door where a bed sheet was stretched in the trees for the screen and several rows of wooden benches were placed directly beneath our window.

For lighting, a single bare light bulb, equipped with a pull string, was hanging at face level. Our bed was a metal four-poster with a lumpy-bumpy mattress of questionable origins and a sheet that should have been in a ragbag.

Down the hallway was a bathroom with a toilet and no seat, and a huge gate valve to flush it. This bathroom satisfied the needs of the entire hotel.

In the bathroom, on a large spike driven into the cement wall, were hanging neatly quarter sections of the *Diario de Yucatán* newspaper that was to be our toilet tissue.

This experience was not for the fainthearted luxury lover, but then this is what true adventures are made of. At least there was this one remaining lodging in Peto for us.

The years have passed and it was time to visit Peto again.

As before, just the trip getting there would make Peto worthwhile.

Today in downtown Peto, traffic is mostly non-motorized, although a new modern highway touches the edge of town.

The train tracks are empty, and the jungle is rapidly disappearing.

Though the pace of life is still unhurried, the noise level has skyrocketed.

Their export economy has changed from chicle and honey to migrant laborers journeying to the U.S. for green-back dollars.

Some of the migrants have returned and have built hotels. So, now there are some modern accommodations in Peto.

Peto speaks volumes of the old and new. This centuries old colonial dwelling is home to a store hawking Chinese imports. *Cositas* = little things.

Mexican military displaying a "show of force" in Peto.

Peto has been a military outpost since the Caste War that began in 1847. The military is still there. Today it is "narcos" to control and not insurgent Mayas.

Our first night in town we found a superbly located hotel in the city center. The bare-bones basic San José is definitely not scrubbed to death but boasts cable television, hammock hooks, and indoor first floor bicycle parking.

We ate well in a *cocina económica* located in the city center. We were fed a huge ration of savory *frijol charros* or pork and beans.

In a *cocina económica* usually one or two dishes are prepared each day, and when they are sold out, the *cocina* closes. You have the choice of eating in or carry-out.

Most of the trade is carry-out. Many households in Yucatan rely on *cocina económicas* for at least one meal each day.

Church on the main plaza in Peto.

Peto's population turns out en masse for community functions like this cheerleader competition that lasted several hours with loud speakers blasting.

Richard Perry in his book *Mayan Missions* gives a lengthy description of the *Virgen de la Estrella* church in Peto. He was not as impressed as we were. We found this to be one of the most formidable and massive ornate examples of dedicated attention to detail that we have encountered in Yucatan. You must come and pass your own judgment.

From the choir loft of the Peto church some perspective can be gained of the mammoth size of this structure that is nearly four meters thick.

The Mayan temple that the materials were salvaged from had to be colossal.

Some of the lumber from Peto's virgin zapote forest wound up in the church. The wood was used for the *vigas* (roof beams) in the side chapels.

Peering down from the bell tower on the front façade, the altitude is breathtaking.

The dizzying height of the roof top is worth the effort, and don't forget your camera!

Looking southwest from the church roof you can easily discern the Puuc hills near to the town of Tekax far off in the distance.

The jungle previously consisted of *zapote* trees from which the *chicle* for chewing gum was extracted. The *zapote* fruit is delicious and savory. It is called sapodilla in English. The *zapote* wood is among the hardest and most enduring of the world. It became irresistible to the greedy timber barons who have harvested the trees to near extinction.

Jane and John on the rooftop of the church at Peto.

As you can see Jane and I go to great lengths to get these interesting stories and photos, especially when you consider that I get dizzy with thick socks on.

All of the building materials for the church were from Mayan temples.

"Is Peto worth a visit?" "Yes."

From Peto a lovely little paved bicycle path leads out of town to a very quiet back road that will take you to Xoy, Chaksinkin, Tixmehuac, and finally Tekax. This is a lovely jungle route past ancient haciendas, tranquil Mayan villages, and intriguing churches.

Another interesting side trip from Peto is to Ichmul.

Ichmul – A Mayan religious center since ancient times.

The present day village of Ichmul is built upon the regional capital of the Cochuah Maya. It was a vital link in the cacao trade. Mounds are visible throughout the village. Five Mayan *sacbe* roads lead out of Ichmul to other former Mayan ceremonial sites.

After the Spanish conquest, Ichmul was a mission town for the Franciscans. Nothing remains of the early mission. Construction began in the late 1700s on the imposing but unfinished church that stands in Ichmul today.

Ichmul church.

The never completed church of Ichmul is a product of the Caste War that doesn't ever seem to go away. A carved stone used in the construction of the church bears a message dating from the days of the ancient Maya.

Nothing of significance has happened in this sleepy town since it was destroyed during the Caste War and abandoned in December of 1847. Only recently have people began to repopulate Ichmul.

Part of the elegant entryway to the church remains.

Surrounding Ichmul are literally thousands of undisturbed Mayan ruins in the jungle that are in the ever so slow process of being pulled down by the vegetation whose roots pry apart the stone work and cause its imperceptible downward fall.

Mexican military on the street in Ichmul.

What is happening in Ichmul hasn't changed much since the Caste War when the military garrison building in the background of the above photo was first occupied. The military is still here. These three soldiers are not as sinister as they appear. They were, in fact, quite friendly and jovial considering the fact that they were on a high alert because of "narcos" operating in the area. Everyone is a suspect in this type of environment, and so we guarded our actions. We didn't want our heads blown off.

The afternoon became hot and eating options in Ichmul were nil, except for hot tortillas, and we already had our fill of them. We decided on a strategy of taking the first transportation out of town no matter which way it was headed (Valladolid or Peto) as it had become too hot to bike and the road too dusty from construction work.

In a few minutes we were seated in air-conditioned comfort and headed back to Peto where we made a miraculous bus connection in less than five minutes of our arrival there to our next destination.

Every day in Mexico is an adventure.

Points of interest in Ichmul:

Unfinished church and *El Santuario* chapel, both with carvings by Pasual Estrella, Mayan ruins, the red military barracks on the small plaza, and well rusted cannons on display from the Caste War era.

At Ichmul at least you don't have to be bothered with hordes of tourists or anybody else. We found out public transportation is limited but still very convenient. We were told that if you bring your own hammock the town officials in the municipal building will let you stay there. No trinket shops or bus tours.

The nearby town of X-Querol, four kilometers south in the adjoining State of Quintana Roo, was and still is occupied by indigenous Maya who have held their ancestral lands to this day. The two towns are linked by a Mayan *sacbe* road that is heavily overgrown by jungle, but passable by horseback or on foot. X-Querol is included in chapter 5: The Church Route.

Ichmul is 37 km east of Peto, 70 km south of Valladolid, and 4 km north of X-Querol.

Getting there:

Buses depart from the ADO stations in both Valladolid and Peto.

Taxis and collective (*colectivo*) vans from Peto or Chikindzonot to Ichmul.

7 - *Yaxcabá, Libre Unión, Tabí, and Sotuta*

A visit to the towns of the Cocom Maya and a distinctive 18th century church.

We made this trip starting at the Noreste bus terminal in downtown Merida but the same trip can be made starting at the ADO bus terminal in Valladolid.

Our second class bus took us on a very sinuous scenic small village route, off the main road.

At eight-thirty we were off-loading at Libre Unión, which is little more than a wide place in the road, some ninety kilometers east of Mérida and fifty-five kilometers west of Valladolid.

Several taxi drivers met the bus and were competing for our business. We had already planned to use whatever type of transport we could to make the next leg of our trip. This was going to be a long action packed day even with the boost of a taxi ride to Yaxcabá.

We were lucky and got a flamboyant taxi driver who was bubbling over with local information.

On the road to Yaxcabá, over grown mounds, which are Mayan temple ruins, lined the way. One of the reasons that this area was so popular with the ancient Maya is that it is a zone of *cenotes* or sinkholes where water was available year-round.

Before 9 a.m. we were on the quiet colonial streets of Yaxcabá. Having our bicycles with us as ground transportation in these interesting out of the way places opens up exploration possibilities you would never get if you travel by automobile or are on foot.

We not only received a convenient ride from Libre Unión to Yaxcabá, but were informed and entertained all the way by our driver, Mario Briceño Dzul.

When we arrived in Yaxcabá, Mario topped off our enjoyable ride by singing a lovely ballad while passionately strumming his guitar.

Mario Briceño Dzul in Yaxcabá.

Although we found that there are many places to eat in Yaxcabá, we had packed along our breakfast, and we ate in the park while quietly watching the city doings.

We watched while a short of stature *campesino* (country man) lugged a large bundle of *leña* (firewood) on his back to cook his day's meals. The high price of cooking gas has forced many here in Yucatan to go to the woods for cooking fuel.

Quiet streets lined with picturesque colonial buildings and a magnificent 18th century church make this out of the tourist loop city well worth a visit for peace loving bicyclers.

San Pedro church, Yaxcabá.

The Yaxcabá church is like none other in Mexico. Inside the recently restored church, its splendor speaks out to you from over the centuries.

Nothing was spared in the restoration of the 1750's original *retablos* that now glisten with glittering gold leaf and meticulously painted deep relief carved figures.

Restored 1750s *retablo*, San Pedro Yaxcabá.

There are six exquisitely restored original side *retablos* in the church. You will definitely want to take the time to view these historical works of art that have survived trial and tribulation plus a long-drawn-out war that was at times centered in Yaxcabá. Also note the artistically painted original wall *frescos* that have survived nearly three centuries.

Over the years Yaxcabá has been a hotbed of armed conflict that fully exploded in 1848 during the Caste War when 5,000 Mayan warriors burst into town. This was on the front lines of that conflict, and Yaxcabá was abandoned by its colonial defenders.

We leave Yaxcabá on this January morning headed into the tranquil back country.

Our next leg of the bicycle trip took us on a quiet rural road through *milpa* (cornfields) country to Tabí. This is a bird watchers paradise and bikers dream come true.

The name Tabí means in Yucatec Maya, the place where there are two *cenotes*.

Tabí is a very quiet Mayan village between Yaxcabá and Sotuta. Both Tabí and Sotuta are seldom visited places with no hotel accommodations and scarcely any eating establishments. However, you won't starve in Tabí. Ask around and someone will prepare you something to eat.

Our Mérida neighbor's mother, Doña Chula, lives in Tabí. We visited with these friendly people, who do not lock their homes and trust their children to roam the streets—something not done in the big city.

The Franciscan church in Tabí is reputed to have one of the finest baroque *retablos* and altar pieces in Yucatan.

Colonial murals and frescos, the most complete sequence in Yucatan, are still in remarkable condition in the Tabí church.

Restoration work has preserved this monumental historical treasure.

Chapel of the Virgin of Tabí.

Tabí has two *cenotes*. One is behind a weathered little stone chapel in the town's center. This cenote has a fanciful legend surrounding it. Legend has it that in the 1600's the Virgin rose up from the waters of the sacred *cenote* in statue form and was deposited in the little chapel there. Then the bells of the chapel began to ring by themselves. The Virgin of Tabí became the entity of a Mayan religious cult.

Inquisitive and smiling children of Tabí.

From Tabí we biked on a very peaceful country road with gentle rolling hills and a significant lack of traffic.

Chapel at entrance to Sotuta.

Entering Sotuta from Tabí, a little chapel that is a relic of the past greets us. This part of the country abounds in such strange curiosities that make for photo-ops.

Sotuta

Our first visit to little Sotuta had been nearly twenty-five years earlier at the end of the thriving henequen era when Sotuta was at the end of the still functional narrow gauge railroad line.

In those days the town was renowned for being the stronghold for a dissident populist movement in Yucatan and even had one of the most powerful radio stations blasting out their independent egalitarian message. The Mexican military maintained a fortified barracks prominently placed on the main city plaza from the beginnings of the Caste War in 1847 that was not relinquished until 1998 when indigenous rights were at a proverbial boiling point. This heightened indigenous rights movement was brought about by the EZLN or the Zapatistas who squared off and took on the Federal government on January 1, 1994, forcing their issue of human rights into international news.

This statue of Nachi Cocom is in the center of Sotuta. A statue of Nachi Cocom was originally placed at the beginning of Paseo de Montejo in Mérida, Yucatan, but was removed because of protests by some non-indigenous residents of Mérida.

Nachi Cocom and Sotuta are synonymous. The Cocom family of Sotuta was one part of the warring Mayan faction that fought against the Xiu family of nearby Maní for centuries after the collapse of their northern empire following a two hundred fifty year drought.

The Spanish conquistadors, after being totally driven out of the Yucatan Peninsula in 1535, returned around 1540 with a new game plan of divide and conquer, and that was to exploit the deep division between the two warring Mayan tribes. This was enough of a tactic to allow the Spanish to get a foothold, and by 1542 they put down roots in T'ho, now known as Mérida.

The palace of Nachi Cocom.

In the center of Sotuta stands a fortress looking building known as the palace of Nachi Cocom. The building now houses a museum and has an interesting but cloudy history. It is obvious that it stands upon a Mayan temple and the structure is constructed from materials taken from it. The dates of subsequent construction at this site are purely conjecture. It is likely that the famous Mayan king Nachi Cocom had a home here when the Spanish took Sotuta in 1542 and made a prisoner of him in 1549. The Spanish built a military barracks at this spot in the 18th century, and it became an armed garrison in 1848, and was occupied by the military until 1998.

17th century Franciscan church in Sotuta.

The Sotuta church began as a Franciscan mission with an open air thatched roof Indian chapel in the mid 1500s. By the 17th century, the present church was completed. Four ornate gold leaf adorned *retablos* dating from 1550 to 1730 can be found in the Sotuta church.

Building on the Sotuta plaza.

83

In Sotuta, traditionally dressed Mayan ladies carry their ground corn home from the *molino* in the style of Yucatan, on their head. This corn is from their own *milpa* farms.

El Goyo of Sotuta.

Friendly old "El Goyo" keeps the city plaza spotlessly tidied up. He showed us his treasured watch, a gift from his 45 year old son that immigrated to the U.S. and seldom returns to visit. Many local families are divided by this economic migration.

Real wealth is found in the smiling faces of these otherwise economically depleted locals.

Tricycle taxis of Sotuta line up at the plaza.

In front of the municipal building non-polluting quiet tricycle taxis queue waiting for clients. The pedal powered tricycle taxis are rapidly being motorized.

Across from the municipal building is located the *cocina económica* where we have lunch each time we revisit the area.

Our no frills lunch spot, Los Arcos, is housed in an ancient colonial building. The owner, Margarita Rejón, and her friend Mirna Cocom* jovially entertain us with hilarious accounts of local happenings, and the food is good.

*Cocom is a family name synonymous with nearly five centuries of Sotuta history.

In the central plaza is a stone bust of Nachi Cocom—still a legend.

Oriente bus terminal in Sotuta, Yucatan.

The bike tour over, I loaded our bicycles aboard the bus back to Mérida, and I got a refreshing snooze along the way.

If you are going back to Valladolid take one of the *colectivo* vans that stop at the small park on the north side of the monument to Nachi Cocom. They will take you to the highway where you can catch a bus to Valladolid.

Getting there:

From Valladolid:
ADO Bus Terminal – Valladolid
Calle 39 on the corner with Calle 46
Oriente bus

From Mérida:
Noreste Bus Terminal – Mérida
Calle 67 between Calle 50 and 52
Oriente bus

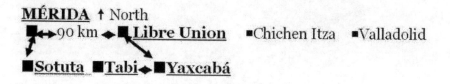

8 - Uayma to Izamal - Travel the Camino Real to Izamal

Izamal, a Side Trip or End Destination.

Until the late 1800s this road was the main and busy Camino Real or royal highway linking the colonial frontier town of Valladolid with Yucatan's capital of Mérida.

Today this route is a quiet back road that takes you through interesting and distinctive Mayan villages on a pleasant and seldom traveled road that links Valladolid with Izamal, ninety kilometers to the west.

This route is ideal because of its reliable public transportation that allows you to incorporate bus and/or biking. We first drove this way in the early 1980s, and it still remains one of our favorites.

If you are interested in distinctive unspoiled sights, which include *cenotes* and colonial era haciendas, this may be just the gem you have been searching for.

Be sure to take your time...especially in Izamal.

Izamal is an ideal departure place for Mérida with excellent bus and taxi service.

Uayma

West twelve kilometers from Valladolid is a one-of-a-kind village nearly forgotten.

Uayma with its painstakingly refurbished 1642 Franciscan church is a place you must visit.

It is close enough to make it a pleasant half day bicycle round trip from Valladolid or incorporate it into a visit on your way on to Izamal and Mérida.

Uayma was a busy town and the last

stop on the Camino Real between Mérida and Valladolid until the late 1800s when a new highway bypassed the town. By the late 1900s even the railroad stopped running through the town, leaving Uayma a quiet forgotten village.

Uayma church.

Inside the church of Uayma.

The church was started by the Franciscans in 1642 and expanded and embellished in the 1800s. The Caste War and the Mexican Revolution left the church in ruins. Several years ago a group from Mérida funded a foundation that restored the church to its former splendor.

Uayma has something rare in this day and time...tranquility.

We love it and take every opportunity we can to enjoy it.

Next to the church there is a park, and nearby is a *cenote* that still supplies the area's water needs.

Don't just pass through this town. Take the time to savor it.

Continuing west ten kilometers toward Izamal, the next town is Tinúm. The centuries old Franciscan church of Tinúm was a victim of the Caste War and remains roofless. Tinúm has a small bakery that uses a wood fired oven. Their breads and pastries are delicious!

At the next town of Dzitás, seventeen kilometers further west, you have the option of diverting south to Pisté and visiting Chichén Itzá.

Remember that you have the option of a bus nearly hourly east or west.

Izamal

As tourist end destinations go, Izamal is one of Yucatan's finest examples of colonial era architecture and well worth your time to explore and get to know.

Izamal, known as the yellow city because most of its buildings are painted yellow, is a lovely colonial town that contains gigantic Mayan temples throughout. Climb to the top of the tallest; the view is spectacular.

Explore the magnificent 1500s church. Tour guides are available at the church and monastery entrance.

Take a carriage ride or tricycle taxi city tour, visit the municipal market, and sample the local foods that range from fine dining to a *cocina económica* where you can get stuffed on local specialties at bargain prices. Souvenir shops abound and real authentic Mexican folk art is here.

Izamal was put on the modern map by a visit from Pope John Paul II in August of 1993. Bishop Fray Diego de Landa put it on the ancient map in the 1500s.

Statue of Bishop Diego de Landa in Izamal.

Izamal has a rich Mayan and conquistador history. Huge temple pyramids are still prominently part of the town. A 16th century Franciscan monastery is situated atop the base of one of them. The statue in the photo above of Bishop Diego de Landa faces the monastery he directed to be built. In July 1562, Friar Diego de Landa held an *auto de fe* Inquisitional ceremony in Maní, burning a number of Maya books and 5000 idols, saying that they were "works of the devil."

The colossal amount of stone harvested from the ancient Mayan temples that stood here to build this city center is simply mind boggling considering that several enormous pyramids still remain standing to this day. We recommend Izamal as a must-see place. Bring your camera, read-up ahead of time, and by all means take a guided carriage ride.

Take your time and spend two or three unhurried days here. It is just too good to hurry through.

Bus and taxi connections on to Mérida and Valladolid are frequent. The bus terminal is located in the downtown area.

Accommodations are numerous. Check Lonely Planet or Moon guide or ask locally.

John L. Stephens in his book *Incidents of Travel in Yucatan*, gives this reflection on his 1840 visit to Izamal:

The eye turned involuntarily to immense mounds rising grandly above the tops of the houses, from which the whole city had been built, without seeming to diminish their colossal proportions, proclaiming the power of those who reared them, and destined, apparently, to stand, when the feebler structures of their more civilized conquerors shall have crumbled into dust.

9 - Chichén Itzá

Chichén Itzá is the largest of the archaeological cities of the pre-Columbian Maya civilization in the Yucatan Peninsula. It was recently selected as one of the New Seven Wonders of the World.

In this book we are pitching the places that tourists miss most.

Chichén Itzá is not one of them.

As a matter of fact Chichén Itzá is unquestionable the most publicized and undoubtedly the most visited attraction in all of México. It has worldwide name recognition and publicity.

"Is it worth a visit?"

My response to that is, "Yes."

Even though the admission fees are very high, visitors are restricted from climbing and entering some areas. Trinket vendors pester, the crowds are overwhelming, and you may be charged extra for video equipment.

So, you have come a long way to see it...you don't need to linger because Yucatan abounds in so many fascinating and interesting things to see and do, and the woods are literally full of Mayan ruins that can be explored without the crowds.

The archeological site of Chichén Itzá is too interesting and controversial to be overlooked.

You have been forewarned.

Location:

40 km from Valladolid

118 km from Mérida

1 km from the village of Pisté

Getting There:

Chichén Itzá is located at the village of Pisté on the Mérida to Cancún highway. There are exits to Chichén Itzá from Mérida-Cancún toll road.

You will find frequent buses to Pisté and many that go directly to the parking lot of Chichén Itzá. Buses depart from the ADO terminal in Valladolid and from three different terminals in Merida: CAME, TAME, and Noreste terminals.

See chapter 19 for more bus information and location of terminals.

10 - Tizimín: A Hub for Exploring Eastern Yucatan

Two hour express bus service to Mérida and half an hour to Valladolid make the out of the tourist loop town of Tizimín an ideal staging place for several seldom visited delightful side trips.

A look at Tizimín

Tizimín's location is extraordinary with excellent eating options and diverse choices in accommodations.

We are no strangers to this one-of-a-kind getaway town. It is linked to Gulf Coast fishing villages, *cenotes*, biosphere reserves, and it is situated in Yucatan's only true cowboy country.

Tizimín, founded in 1553, has a population of 46,971 (2010 census) and is one of the largest cities in eastern Yucatan. Tizimín, whose Mayan name means place of the tapir, is a quiet easy going and friendly town central to the many dairy farms and area cattle ranches.

Church of Los Santos Reyes de Tizimín.

In the center of the city is located the 16th century Los Santos Reyes de Tizimín (Church of the Three Kings) and its former Franciscan monastery. They are worth a visit.

The church is outwardly spartan, but inwardly mammoth and ornately adorned with interesting gilded statuary, the most impressive being the glass cases containing the three kings or *Los Santos Reyes de Tizimín.*

Restoration within produced some photo opportunities.

Three Kings Day is celebrated on January 6 of every year in Mexico. In Tizimín the celebration is a fair and festival that lasts two weeks and starts the end of December.

Nights the parks have a wonderful selection of street vendors selling Mexican traditional foods that include a wide variety of exquisite *tamales.*

We have been coming here for nearly thirty years and continue to be pleasantly surprised by this unique town in Yucatan's cattle country.

One of our greatest pleasures in travel is finding foods we love to eat. Having said that, on Calle 47 adjacent to the IMSS hospital is Sariah, an all natural bakery featuring whole wheat and other natural products...their delicious goods at low prices will make you wish that you had purchased even more of their wholesome products.

Also on Calle 47 and directly across from the bus terminal is one of many good bicycle repair shops...they have a selection of parts from cheap to top quality.

The Tizimín municipal market is not to be missed. It isn't huge or expansive, but it is very clean and features some of Yucatan's finest Mexican and Mayan specialty foods that change with the seasons: *polkanes, tortitas de chaya, zapotitos,* and *ish waaj,* and much more.

This vendor in the photo on the right is selling cornbread and *ish waaj, Ish waaj* is a thin flat cracker, either salt or sugar flavored, available seasonally from new corn.

John is chatting with women selling *polkanes*, *ish waaj*, and flowers at the Tizimín market.

A few words of Maya and a smiling face go a long way in cementing a friendly atmosphere. These are friendly people and love to joke.

At the Tizimín market we stock up on all the delectable specialties that we can carry off, and when we get home we always wish we had purchased even more.

You may get the impression that all we enjoy is finding something interesting to eat. Well, in Yucatan if you don't partake of the outstanding selection of local specialty foods you are missing the boat on travel adventures here.

The Tizimín area is prosperous and growing rapidly. Bus and taxi service is excellent to Valladolid, Mérida, and area towns.

Biking north and east of Tizimín is best in early mornings with the offshore sea breeze. Easterly midmorning onshore winds build through the afternoon. Take advantage of these winds and put the sun on your back with a tail wind.

History at a glance: Looking back at Tizimín.

In the book *Incidents of Travel in Yucatan* published in 1842, the author, John Stephens listed the following as export items from Tizimín: tortoise shell, skins, timber, logwood, India-rubber, incense, tobacco, *achiote* (a substitute for saffron and a very rich dye), starch from the *yucca*, cotton, wax, honey, molasses, sugar, rum, castor oil, salt, amber, vanilla, hogs, and cochineal.

According to British Admiralty charts from that time, the northern coastal area of Yucatan was densely forested with 70-foot tall mahogany and *zapote* trees. That solid forest survived over three hundred years of Spanish occupation but would not survive another century. The tropical timber completely vanished into three lumber mills at nearby Colonia Yucatán. Conservation and replanting were not in this equation. Today the timber has been replaced by dairy farming and cattle ranching.

Posada Pastora, located on Calle 51 between Calle 52 and Calle 54, is a quiet and pleasant lodging. They have off-street parking, and they are bicycle friendly. The bus terminal and municipal market are nearby.

The twenty first century may have arrived, but it hasn't impacted Tizimín totally. At the bus terminal you can still hire a hand drawn cargo cart to lug your luggage home.

First and second class buses are in the city center. See end of chapter for more bus information.

Side Trips from Tizimín

Las Coloradas

Mounds of sea salt at Las Coloradas waiting for shipment. Photo courtesy Felipe González, Hotel Villa de Pescadores, Rio Lagartos.

Michael D. Coe, in his book, *The Maya*, wrote about Las Coloradas, one of the salt sources of the early Maya. The following is excerpted from his book:

Happily, the greatest salt sources in all Mesoamerica lie within the Maya area. The major one consisted of the salt beds along lagoons of Yucatan's north coast. There, grids of shallow, rectilinear pens (still in use) allowed the lagoon water to evaporate during the dry season. Once a thick layer of salt had hardened; it was raked up and transported in baskets. On the eve of the Conquest, these beds were controlled by Yucatan's most powerful kingdoms, and their product was traded to places as distant as the Rio Pánuco in northern Veracruz.

Las Coloradas, with a population of about 1,000, is a coastal village in north central Yucatan within the Biosphere Reserve of Ria Lagartos. The topography consists of a unique coastal ecosystem of mangroves, dunes and lagoons. This area is semiarid making it ideal for solar dehydrating sea salt. Sea salt production has been done here since ancient Mayan times when huge trading canoes transported this heavy product to distant ports of Central America, Florida, and Veracruz. Today that production continues and the product is loaded into trucks and ships. Las Coloradas can be reached by bus from Tizimín and Rio Lagartos. There are accommodations at nearby Rio Lagartos. Bicycling is good with limited but quiet roads.

Ek Balam Archeological Site

If you have time constraints and want to beat the crowds to Ek Balam, consider taking the bus from Tizimín to Ek Balam. See chapter 11 – Ek Balam.

Rio Lagartos and Sendero Peten Tucha

Rio Lagartos is a coastal tourist fishing village 56 km north of Tizimín, 95 km north of Valladolid and 230 km from Mérida. A layover of two or three days on this quiet loop trip to the Gulf of Mexico makes it better. Off season is best. Avoid

July-August and Easter week. The ultimate off season for best weather with no tourists is September-December.

This trip can be made by bike or bus. If you wish to bike and have time constraints or prefer a more leisurely trip, take the bus from Tizimín to Panabá and then bike the 30 kilometers to San Felipe.

Hire a boat to take you to the beach for a swim, and later bike on another 12 km to Rio Lagartos. Another consideration is to get an early start on your bike before the onshore sea breeze that begins near 10 a.m. This wind can be used to your advantage when returning from Rio Lagartos where you will want to spend at least one night. To return to Tizimín you can take the bus or bike the 56 kilometers. See chapter 12 - Rio Lagartos.

Tizimín to Colonia Yucatán and El Cuyo

Take the bus from Tizimín to Colonia Yucatán and then El Cuyo or bike the last 38 kilometer stretch to El Cuyo from Colonia Yucatán. It is one of the loveliest areas for a bicycle trip...this rural Yucatan road is best done early morning. If you feel adventurous, after you spend a night or two in El Cuyo, bicycle the dirt 50 kilometer beach road west to Rio Lagartos passing Las Coloradas. Be warned: There are no facilities along the beach front road. See chapter 13 - El Cuyo.

Dzilám de Bravo

Biking the 107 kilometer seldom traveled rural back road takes you to Panabá, Santa Rosa, Yalsihón, Yashilón and on to Dzilám de Bravo, the old pirate strong hold. Be warned; Dzilám de Bravo does not have decent overnight accommodations but is an interesting fishing village proud of its link to the pirate Lafitte. There is a bay front monument to the pirate.

The nearby town of Dzilám González has bus service to Tizimín. There are several buses a day from Dzilám de Bravo to Mérida. See Chapter 15 – Buctzotz and on to Dzilám.

Getting to Tizimin from Valladolid

ADO Bus Terminal

Calle 39 and the corner of Calle 46

Getting to Tizimín from Mérida

Autobuses del Noreste Terminal

Calle 67 betweens Calle 50 and 52

Noreste has several first class direct buses a day to Tizimín, plus many second class buses. If you want to see the sights, take the second class bus. It meanders through many villages before arriving many hours later in Tizimín.

If you want a fast comfortable trip, take the Noreste direct bus that makes frequent trips daily to Tizimín. The trip takes two hours. The first class buses have toilets; the second class buses do not.

Leaving Tizimín

Tizimín Bus Terminals

Autobuses del Noreste Terminal

Calle 47 on the corner with Calle 46

First class and second class bus service to Mérida and points in between. There is also service to Cancun and Tulum.

This is where you get the second class bus to San Felipe and Rio Lagartos.

ADO Terminal

Calle 46 between Calle 45 and 47

First and second class bus service to Mérida, Cancún, and Valladolid.

11 - Ek Balam Mayan Archeological Site and Temozón

Ek Balam is one of the most imposing Mayan archeological sites in the Yucatan with elaborately carved sculptures and richly adorned temples and plazas.

The recently restored Mayan ruins of Ek Balam are best visited from nearby Valladolid or Tizimín. You can take a bus or local taxi or make it a fascinating bicycle trip. Plan to arrive at Ek Balam at 8 a.m., when they open, to avoid crowds and beat the heat.

Consider taking your bike one way by taxi to arrive early ahead of the crowd. After you have completed your tour, a leisurely return trip with stops for eats and refreshments makes for a memorable experience. The view from atop the main pyramid is spectacular. Bring your camera, photo opportunities abound.

There are accommodations nearby in the village of Ek Balam.

On our visit to Ek Balam, Jane and I wanted to share a special moment alone at this incredible landmark of ancient Mayan heritage. We had an early morning breakfast, and then we put our bicycles in the trunk of a taxi and arrived at

Ek Balam ahead of the competition and captured a priceless memory.

A view from the top of the pyramid of Ek Balam.

Tranquility and splendor are here. Recently reclaimed from the encroaching jungle, these monumental achievements of ancient Mayan glory cry out across the millennium and tell us of a proud civilization.

This is the famous Mayan *corbelled* arch.

The grounds of Ek Balam are meticulously kept, and restoration is progressing at a measured pace that is not disruptive to visitors.

Walk around behind some of the ruins and you get a glimpse of what Ek Balam looked like before archeological renovation began and reclaimed the magnificent Mayan buildings that have been the victim of neglect for the past four-hundred and fifty plus years. At least they were not quarried to build cathedrals, which was the fate of so many of these temples that are now lost for all time.

Beating the crowd paid big dividends. Peace and quiet are priceless commodities in this world of go-fast jet-setting...so, come and enjoy this gift of the ancient Maya.

Our bicycle ride back to Valladolid took us down a quiet seldom traveled back road that passed through the poor little Mayan village of Santa Rita where we found a park and shade trees to enjoy our morning coffee. Dogs, pigs, and chickens roamed through the park and were undisturbed by the nuisance of city traffic or commotion in this quiet rural setting.

After our break, we biked down the road to Temozón, a bustling town that was on our way back to Valladolid.

This is the heart of downtown Temozón.

In the Temozón market we were treated to a scrumptious and very ample meal prepared by the lady who owned and operated her own home style kitchen.

Visiting places like Temozón make cross country bicycling rewarding and memorable.

Sights along the way; Moctezuma is pointing the way to Valladolid. We were ready to find any shade on this sun-blistering afternoon.

Getting there:

There are frequent buses from Valladolid and Tizimin.

Bicycle rentals are available in Valladolid from Mexigotours located behind the cathedral on Calle 43, No. 204c between Calle 40 and 42.

12 - Rio Lagartos

Rio Lagartos is a picturesque coastal fishing village on Yucatan's Gulf Coast ninety-five kilometers north of Valladolid, forty-six kilometers from Tizimín, and 230 kilometers from Mérida, Yucatan. The name, Rio Lagartos, implies river of lizards, but there are no rivers in Yucatan. This is a bay or *ciénaga* protected by a barrier island. There are, however, lots of crocodiles.

Rio Lagartos is situated within the 60,000 hectare *Reserva de La Biosfera Ria Lagartos* (Ria Lagartos Biosphere Reserve). The topography is low coastal scrub, mangrove salt marshes, expansive lagoons, sand spit barrier islands, sandy beaches, and fresh water springs.

East of the lighthouse and at the end of the waterfront boulevard is a large fresh water spring known as an *ojo de aqua* and a rustic picnic park.

Photo is of the *ojo de agua* park.

Most travelers come here for the guided boat tours that include; lagoon excursions, bird watching, viewing seasonal migrating birds, sea turtle observations, Mayan curative mud baths, fly-fishing expeditions, and nocturnal crocodile watching. Most guides speak English. If you arrive by bus more than likely a guide will approach you at the terminal.

Rio Lagartos: View of the lagoon and lighthouse.

The *faro* or lighthouse with its distinctive group "three" flashing light is a prominent landmark situated on a point along the waterfront boulevard (Malecón). The Malecón extends along the entire length of the village. A navigable marked channel traverses the shallow bay out into the Gulf of Mexico.

Hotel Villa de Pescadores. Photo courtesy Felipe González, Hotel Villa de Pescadores, Rio Lagartos.

Hotel Villa de Pescadores is as waterfront as you can get and surrounded by expansive wildlife reserves along the Gulf of Mexico. It is one of Rio Lagartos most appealing hotels.

From your room you have a panoramic view of the entire bay, lighthouse, inlet, and fresh natural air flow that is worth more than the trip all by itself. An all day procession of aquatic birds silently gliding past on the gentle sea breezes adds a priceless touch of nature to this special place. A spacious private balcony, hammock ready, along with tranquility is hard to find in this day and time. The management, Felipe González and his lovely wife Elena, treat you like long lost friends, not just paying clients.

Sunrises and sunsets on the northern coast of Yucatan are distinctively enhanced by occurring over the Gulf of Mexico waters. In Rio Lagartos almost all of the sunsets are spectacular.

The fall season has the local fishing fleet outfitted for *pulpo* or octopus fishing.

A special treat for us while visiting the seashore is to prepare our own *ceviche*. We carry a small cutting board and a sharp knife, spoons and forks...all that is needed.

At the local market we buy limes, an onion, tomato, and chili pepper – serrano, jalapeño or habanero. In the afternoon we purchase a fish fresh from the fishermen, fillet cut it in very thin slices and place it in a plastic bag or bowl along with chopped tomato, diced onion, and chili pepper (cilantro is a good addition to *ceviche* but hard to sanitize on the road). Liberally squeeze lime juice over this mixture. It is ready when the fish flesh turns white, and it is delicious. Eat on soda crackers or with tortilla chips.

This delicious meal is convenient, requires no cooking, and it can be prepared with limited equipment.

This recipe works equally well with almost all seafood...just make sure it is fresh!

A tour to see the flamingos is well worth the time it takes. There is no shortage of tourist guides and all newcomers are soon approached. If you can get a group of four or five the price of these boat tours can be split for a substantial savings.

White pelicans find their way to Rio Lagartos every year.

The white pelicans are silent giants equal in size to the great California condor. They are graceful and powerful flyers with a nine foot wing span and among the world's largest aquatic birds.

They migrate each fall from as far north as the Hudson Bay of northern Canada all the way here to Yucatan. Unlike their brown pelican relatives, these huge birds do not dive for their fish, but they wade in shallow water using their large bill as a fishing scoop.

Northern Yucatan's tidal estuaries are home to thousands of pink flamingos. Their distinctive pink color is a result of a diet rich in salt flat marine creatures that impart pink pigment to the birds. They appear larger than they are because of gangly legs and an extremely long neck. Adults have a 60-inch wing span, and they are forty-six inches in length.

Seldom seen alone, flamingos fish together and they fly in flocks. They can often be seen at dusk and at dawn flying along the coast, often offshore. Flamingos are not noisy birds but do occasionally honk similar to geese.

The coast of Yucatan has bird watching at its finest. Sea birds, shore birds, salt flat birds, fresh water birds, and jungle birds abound here. Be sure to bring your camera and take lots of photos...it is a great sport.

To avoid crowds and competition for facilities, off season is the best time to visit Rio Lagartos, and it also happens to coincide with the finest weather. September to mid-December is your time.

There is frequent taxi and bus service from Rio Lagartos to Tizimín with connections to Mérida, Valladolid, Cancún, and Tulum. There is also bus service to the nearby fishing village of San Felipe and to Los Coloradas, a sea salt production town established countless centuries ago in ancient Mayan times.

Where to Stay

Villa de Pescadores
Malecón and Calle 14
Rio Lagartos, Yucatan
www.hotelriolagartos.com.mx

Budget accommodation in Rio Lagartos
Cabañas Las Escondidas
Next door to the restaurant Isla Contoy on the waterfront.

Recommended Guides

Ismael Navarro

Elmer Canul Yam

Fishing guide, bird guide, guide to the *Reserva de La Biosfera Ria Lagartos* Isla Contoy Restaurant Rio Lagartos riolaga@hotmail.com Cel. 986 866 5213

Fly fishing guide, bird guide, guide to the *Reserva de La Biosfera Ria Lagartos* Elmer_flamingos@hotmail.com Cel. 986 866 7318

Side Trip to Sendero Peten Tucha

Visit *Sendero Peten Tucha* at the *Reserva de La Biosfera Ria Lagartos.*

This coastal region of northern Yucatan is home to two expansive wildlife reserves, *Reserva Ecológica Bocas de Dzilám* and *Reserva de la Biosfera Ria Lagartos.*

The area of the reserves is sparsely populated and has good quiet roads with several interesting places to visit.. You can visit this area by car, bus or taxi, but cycling is by far the most rewarding, especially with the wind on your back.

Remember that this is the land of take it easy, and afternoons in Yucatan were designed especially for hammocks and *siestas.*

On the seldom traveled road from Rio Lagartos to Las Coloradas and between kilometers eight and nine, there is a culvert and nearby a small sign denoting fifty meters to the entrance of the hiking path *Sendero Peten Tucha* (A sendero is a walking path. A *peten* is low land known as a hammock that emerges from the marsh. Tucha is a monkey).

If you are looking for the perfect unspoiled wetlands getaway
with no tour buses or trinket shops, this is for you. In the
photo Jane stands before a *palapa* located at the entrance to
the trail where you may relax and refresh in the welcome
tranquil shade.

This is a wetlands walking
tour. We did, however, take
our bicycles although we
had to walk in several
places. Along the trail you
will find numerous well
shaded benches where the
tropical forest ambiance
can be appreciated to the
fullest.

The sign warns: *No nadar – cuidado – cocodrilos* (Do not
swim – caution – crocodiles).

The footpath, (*sendero*) divides around a huge open fresh water spring. One side of the foot path is on an elevated boardwalk through the wetlands of a mangrove hammock. The other side is a smooth well shaded pathway and both converge at a tall observation tower that commands a magnificent view.

At the end of the trail is a pond that is actually a flowing fresh water spring. It is home to crocodiles that only make their presence known when you tempt them by swimming in their private pond.

Climb the viewing tower situated at one side of the pond, and you may spot a crocodile, some turtles, or tropical birds, or hear the call of a *tucha* (Mayan word for monkey).

This is a small slice of the unspoiled Yucatan that tourists miss most...we love it.

Side trip to San Felipe, Yucatan

In spite of the modern road that links Rio Lagartos to San Felipe, the traffic is nearly nonexistent.

It makes a particularly nice bicycle ride, especially in early mornings with the sun and wind at your back.

San Felipe cemetery.

On the only road entering San Felipe the immaculately kept cemetery with its dazzling adornments of colorful plastic flowers is worthy of your scrutiny.

San Felipe makes an interesting stopover on the way to somewhere else. This is only a fishing village not geared to tourism or travelers. The only hotel has a lack luster attitude with no off season rates. Finding something to eat is the same story.

There was one thing that could be of interest; a boat ride across the bay to the Gulf of Mexico beach could be procured for one hundred pesos, and the guide said he would wait for you up to one hour for that price.

San Felipe's waterfront street is very low key and extremely clean and well maintained.

Check out the wooden cottages. The wooden siding is comprised of boards more than eighteen inches wide. These boards were harvested here and are either mahogany or zapote. When the timber barons finished clear cutting the virgin forest that stood here they didn't leave a tree for a bird to sit in...the birds had to hop around on the ground...that was fifty years ago.

From San Felipe you have the option of an alternate route back to Tizimín. The route is a good choice, especially if you chose to bicycle it. The narrow road has little traffic and passes through Panabá on the way into Tizimín.

San Felipe does have one significant claim to fame.

This was the seaport for Chichén Itzá in Mayan times and was linked by a paved sacbe road.

For more side trips from Rio Lagartos, see chapter 10, Tizimín: A Hub for Exploring Eastern Yucatan.

13 - El Cuyo and Colonia Yucatán

We have discovered the mysterious vanishing Mayan temples of El Cuyo.

Colonia Yucatán

Colonia Yucatán has nothing to entice the passer-by to even slow down for except a couple of speed bumps.

This is the heart of the downtown business district with the municipal building on the left where the entire police force soaks up the tranquility in the "nothing happens" shade.

The ancient Maya had several temples here that were mostly salvaged for their stone, but not much worthy of mention happened until the area's towering mahogany and *zapote* forests were noticed.

The British Admiralty chart dating from 1840 tells much of the story of this out-of-the-way place. At the time of the 1840 chart publication, Yucatan had been under Spanish domination for nearly three-hundred years and the Yucatecans were in the process of arming the Mayan Indians to keep the Mexicans out under governor Barbachano who was a separatist and formerly of the neighboring state of Campeche. Yucatan had also contracted with the Texas Navy to patrol their coast for a monthly fee of $8.000 to ensure their sovereignty.

The chart reveals that the barrier peninsula had one hut and six Mayan ruins visible as aids to navigation, one of which was one-hundred feet high. The chart also shows the peninsula was forested with trees sixty feet tall and across on the mainland the trees were seventy feet tall. There were no roads and the place known then as *Rachel* is approximately where present day Colonia Yucatán is located.

Less than ten years after this chart was printed the Yucatan was plunged into their Caste War that lasted nearly sixty years. In this period of time clear-cut deforestation began in this area and lasted until the 1950s when the last mahogany tree was hacked down. The timber barons are a very efficient lot. The saw mills of Colonia Yucatán fell silent when the trees were all gone and bustling Colonia Yucatán became a quiet wide place in the road on the way to somewhere else.

Waiting for the bus in Colonia Yucatán.

Colonia Yucatán has no hotels or regular restaurants and their bus terminal is part of a variety store with the waiting room situated on the street front patio.

The British Admiralty chart of 1840 clearly shows our next destination as *Monte Cuyo Artificial Mound*. That artificial mound happens to be one of the former Mayan temples that eventually evolved into the base for El Cuyo's light house. Further west along the coast the chart notes numerous "*peaks*" that were all Mayan ruins.

The thirty-eight kilometer road north to El Cuyo is picturesque and the best suited for bicycling that we have found in northern Yucatan.

John L. Stephens in his book *Incidents of Travel in Yucatan* describes El Cuyo as he viewed it from seaward when he returned from a month long Caribbean investigational voyage in a sailing vessel in 1840:

The coast was low, barren, and monotonous. At three o'clock we passed an ancient mound, towering above the huts that constituted the port of El Cuyo, a landmark for sailors, visible at sea three leagues distant.

This is downtown El Cuyo with its limited attractions. Behind me is the little church, and further back is the lighthouse prominently perched upon the remains of an ancient Mayan temple. The town has no stop lights, and there are no tourists except for two weeks around Easter and then again for six weeks in July and August when it is packed.

The accommodations are numerous and range from two-star modest to zero-star stark; so take your pick. If you come off season, which accounts for ten months of the year, you can choose any room in town that suits your fancy.

El Cuyo's fishermen's harbor.

Just west of town is the little protected fishermen's harbor that seems to still be hauling in fish, and it is just about the last place on the Yucatan peninsula where fish are plentiful.

Sunrise in El Cuyo.

Here at Latitude 21.5 ° N. in June, we were more than two degrees south of the sun.

On the lagoon side of the island gossamer clouds are reflected in the glassy sunrise stillness.

Jane on the El Cuyo causeway.

Looking south from El Cuyo the substantial elevated causeway stretches off to one of the most beautiful stretches of roadway in northern Yucatan. Jane casts long shadows while the early morning sun creeps up over the Gulf of Mexico where it is actually north of our latitude this time of year.

The British Admiralty chart dating from 1840 shows two significant things. One there was no causeway back in 1840, and secondly several Mayan temples were depicted as high mounds visible from the sea. The mysterious disappearance of those Mayan ruins could only be accounted for by this colossal causeway stretching off across this huge lagoon, and the building materials to build the town of El Cuyo.

El Cuyo lighthouse.

El Cuyo lighthouse is definitely an eye catching allure that beckons you to explore. It is perched atop the remains of an ancient Mayan temple.

At the time of our visit Capt. Russell Rene Garcia Sanchez was the harbor master and held the keys to the lighthouse.

As Capt. Russell handed me the keys, his parting advice was to be extra careful on the stairs.

The view from the top of the lighthouse is spectacular.

Looking northwest from the top of the El Cuyo lighthouse.

This is not the worst of the stairs leading up to the top of the lighthouse.

Capt. Russell grossly understated his warning to be careful on the stairs. It was a frightening experience when I was half way up to discover that the stair treads that were intact were rotten to the core, and I was committed to complete my trip to the top just to turn around.

It is refreshing today to find a tropical beach still nearly deserted with no traffic lights or pushy traffic to contend with, and we truly appreciated the slow pace with the easy going atmosphere at El Cuyo.

Like my favorite German author Herman Hesse said, "Not for everybody."

14 - *Buctzotz to Dzilám González, Dzidzantún, and Pirates*

Half way from Mérida to Tizimín is located the quaint seldom visited town of Buctzotz. If no tourist traps, traffic lights or franchise eateries are your preference, this is for you. The semiarid nondescript topography is a low flat plain of sparsely wooded scrub. Heading west from here across the rest of northern Yucatan, it is the same. It makes for fine bicycling on the seldom traveled back roads. Points of interest are pirates, small colonial Spanish towns, churches, haciendas, and Mayan temple ruins.

Buctzotz church.

Every time we encounter one of these ancient colonial period Spanish churches we automatically have to think back to the great Mayan temples that went to furnish their building materials. The Spanish conquistadors were great recyclers.

The church is one of a few stacked stone buildings from colonial times that still has its roof intact.

Interior of Buctzotz church.

What holds up these stone roofs are wooden *vigas* that are exposed in the church's ceiling.

Even if these *vigas* are made from the most enduring wood, if moisture is allowed to dampen them, they will sooner or later fall victim to rot and cause an avalanche of tons of stone destroying the roof and killing anyone unfortunate enough to be caught under the bombardment.

Every rainy season in Yucatan many of these old structures become saturated.

Even a bird's nest blocking up a roof drain can cause huge amounts of water to compound the weight of the already very heavy roof, and down they come.

Civic pride is apparent everywhere you look, and the conspicuous lack of motorized traffic makes us long for those tranquil times in bygone years.

The main plaza in Buctzotz is clean and well shaded. It is a perfect place to partake of the unhurried pace of life that seems to have escaped the rest of the world.

Quiet streets coupled with a clean and well maintained town are rare treasures these days.

This smiling foursome greeted us with more questions than a thousand wise men could answer.

For copious quantities of savory Yucatecan style cuisine, we hit the jack-pot here in an unpretentious restaurant, *Lol-Beh,* across from the municipal market and less than one block from the central park. We managed to get stuffed beyond capacity.

Our choice of hotels is simple; there is only one in town.

The Posada Nicte-Ha was just great for us. The clean rooms had beds, hammock hooks, and natural cross ventilation.

Nicte-Ha in the Mayan language means water lily.

The antiquated but adequate accommodations brought back to us many fond memories from our first adventures across Yucatan in the days of rail travel.

Where in the world can you find streets devoid of traffic these days? Come to the outback of Yucatan and see for yourself!

Photo: Dzilám González church.

After a peaceful night in Buctzotz, we made an early morning departure. Jane and I cycled northwest out of town into the open countryside still wet from the previous night's downpour caused by a tropical wave. The air was cool and fresh, but the humidity was so dense it felt like we were biking into a wall of water.

Our next stop was at Dzilám González, a picturesque colonial town south of Dzilám de Bravo.

Dzilám González

Looking west out of the main doors of the church in Dzilám González, it is apparent that even with over four hundred years of looting materials from the Mayan temple across the street, it still presents a formidable presence.

The towering pile of stone remains a powerful reminder of the ancient Maya and their homeland.

"Where is all the traffic?"

"Where are all the people?"

This is not off-season in Dzilám González because there is no tourist season here and this kind of quiet tranquility would drive many to positive distraction. We enjoy it just the same knowing that there is still someplace on the planet like this, off the main road, that we can easily get to by bike and bus from our home.

From Dzilám González it is only twelve kilometers to the Gulf of Mexico and Dzilám de Bravo, a small and quiet fishing village where the coconut plantation lined coastal road east of Progreso ends. The pirate Jean Lafitte and the ancient sea salt beds of the Maya made it famous.

Piracy was the scourge of colonial Yucatan, the Caribbean Sea and the Gulf of Mexico.

From the beginning of Spanish occupation of America, pirates ravaged their shipping. Gold looted from the Indigenous Americans being shipped back to Spain proved an irresistible treasure.

French and English kings encouraged and sanctioned these privateers, making contracts with them specifying the division of the spoils.

Buccaneers John Hawkins, Frances Drake, Henry Morgan, William Parker, Laurens de Graff, Henri de Gramond, Jean Lafitte, and Pierre Lafitte were well known in the area and their exploits legendary.

Dzidzantún, Campeche, Tihosuco, Valladolid, and Bacalar were some of the towns that the pirates brazenly conquered and occupied. Many of the pirates took up residency with families on Yucatan's desolate northern coast and along the Caribbean Sea. A story is told that Jean Lafitte is buried at the Gulf of Mexico coastal town of Dzilám de Bravo, Yucatan.

John L. Stephens visited Dzilám de Bravo in 1840. He had heard rumors of Lafitte's death and inquired of the villagers: *At eight o'clock I reached the village...all knew of his death (Lafitte) and burial, but none knew or cared to tell where he was laid. We had heard, also, that his widow was living in the place, but this was not true. There was, however, a negress who had been a servant to the latter, and who, we were told, spoke English; the cura sent for her, but she was so intoxicated that she could not make her appearance.*

The following is from the *Diario de Yucatán* newspaper July 9, 1960. The headline read: "LA TUMBA DE JEAN LAFITTE" (The Tomb of Jean Lafitte). The article states: *Mr. Luis H. González, representative of the Club of Explorers and Sports Archeologists of México, (CEDAM) informed us that they will present a plaque on the 20th of this month and dedicate it at the tomb of the pirate Jean Lafitte in the town of Dzilám de Bravo. The plaque will be dedicated by club founder and president Pablo Bush Romero, a prestigious hunter and sportsman, in cooperation with the Caribbean Archeological and Exploring Society, the Middle American*

*Archeological Society and the Yucatan Exploring Society,
and important archeological societies of the United States.*

July 20, 1960, photo of dedication. Pictured from left: unknown, Mr. Gowen, Clara Gowen, Pablo Bush Romero, Luis H. González, Alma Reed, and unknown person. Photo courtesy of Luis H. González.

Luis H. González contributed the stone to which the plaque is attached. The stone had been a González family grave marker.

Speculation interspersed with myth and rumor spiced with unsubstantiated historical facts have made Jean Lafitte legendary.

On to Dzidzantún

Biking out of Dzilám González, our next stop was at Dzidzantún whose name means gleaming precious stone in Maya.

This ancient town of the Chel Maya had a *sacbe* road linking it to the coast. They prospered from their sea salt beds with a lucrative trade until the Spanish conquered. In the mid 1600s French and English pirates sacked Dzidzantún.

Dzidzantún church.

The fortress sized church, dedicated in 1567 and completed by 1580, was the largest in 16th century Yucatan, and the longest in Mexico; it measures 250 feet inside from door to altar. Even neglected the roof did not cave in until 1908. It was restored by the 1980s.

We have passed the huge church structure often, each time exclaiming that one day we would return to investigate. The book *Mayan Missions* by Richard Perry finally got us there.

The frescos inside the church were recently restored and refurbished. Take a close look at the exotic art work depicting caricatures of animal/human faces, like the dog's face sporting horns and human eyes. This is fascinating stuff that may have been painted by Mayan artists centuries ago.

It staggers the imagination to contemplate the massive size of the Mayan temple required to furnish the materials for this enormous church. This is an immense monument, and it is well worth a visit.

It is not possible to do justice to this incredible building completely constructed of stacked stone.

The adjacent cloister, which is but a small part of the building complex, is colossal.

Come take a look for yourself.

Well in Dzidzantún.

In the town of Dzidzantún were located many distinct water wells with their large cylindrical cone topped gantry supports used to fasten the pulleys for retrieving the water.

This style well was unique to Dzidzantún and now a large old hacienda, San Francisco, is being restored adjacent to Dzidzantún, and the wells are a part of that project.

From Dzidzantún we took the bus to our next destination.

Dzidzantún has frequent bus service to Mérida, Tizimín, and points in between.

Our excursion from Buctzotz to Dzidzantún was a lovely out of the tourist loop trip. There is nothing quite like Yucatan for the adventure traveler.

15 - Tulum - The Mexican Caribbean's Best Beach

Relax and swim at the Mexican Caribbean's best public beach: Santa Fe, located south of the Tulum Mayan ruins.

You might get the impression that the Riviera Maya and the Caribbean Sea are just about fun in the sun and beaches. The salubrious crystal clear water is comfortable year round making water sports a worldwide draw. Tulum is blessed with the best of the best in this department. The offshore coral reef, one of the world's largest, calms the waves making swimming, snorkeling, and scuba diving an unforgettable experience...not for everybody. Surfers go to the Pacific coast.

The very best of these beaches is the one that starts at the majestic Mayan ruins perched high atop a rock outcropping and runs south for three kilometers. Heavenly shade is provided by coconut palms and sea grape trees...ideal for swinging hammocks. Public access signs are posted.

Tulum is more than just a beach: eateries and accommodations abound.

Discover real Mexican food out of the tourist loop.

After you have surveyed Avenida Tulum, the main street, with its carnival atmosphere complete with persistent hawkers pitching everything from trinkets to tattoos and the countless restaurants, go to the traffic circle corner by the Scotia Bank.

On the street of Satelite Sur vendors of Mexican food begin in early morning and change over the day and evening.

The *antojitos* are excellent and at reasonable rates.

Wikipedia defines an *antojito* as a Mexican street snack designed to satisfy a craving. Many *antojitos* have become icons of Mexican cuisine, such as the *tamales*, and can be found in almost every region of Mexico.

In Yucatan, *antojitos* are eaten for breakfast and in the evening. The main meal in Mexico is *el almuerzo* or *la comida* that is eaten at midday. Many *antojitos* are large and substantial and can easily replace a meal. *Tacos, tortas* (sandwiches) *empanadas, quesadillas, huaraches, gorditas, salbutes, panuchos, tamales, perros calientes* (hot dogs) and *hamburguesas* (hamburgers) are all *antojitos*.

A mini restaurant on wheels.

Antojitos in the style of Mexico City.

The best of real Mexican regional food directly from Mexico City is prepared here by Dolores, the owner and a recent arrival in Tulum. She will make you feel like part of her family after your first visit.

This is true street food served on the sidewalk.

John and Dolores.

Smiling Jane is about to savor half an order of *huarache,* a Mexico City specialty.

The name *huarache* is that of a type of a Mexican shoe, and the owner of this eating establishment, Dolores, has a very tall son with big feet...she patterned her delicious *huaraches* after the size of his feet.

The *tamales* arrive on the street around six in the evening.

Evenings the *tamale* vendor on Satelite Sur will add as much hot chili sauce as your gastronomy can tolerate.

These *tamales* are a style of the Mexico City area where corn husks are used to wrap them for steaming. The Yucatan style employs banana leaves.

One of my favorite Mexican style *tamales* is *mole con pollo*. Jane loves the vegetarian *tamale* of *rajas con queso*.

Mexico boasts over a thousand different varieties of *tamales*...too good to quit. Self restraint can be nearly impossible with these eats, which can easily become an addictive substance. It is easy to go home resembling a short stack of *tortillas*. The variety of *tacos* is much the same case, and Tulum has some of the most savory of all.

Another place where good and economical food can be found is on the southern end of the main street around the corner on Calle Jupiter. The food court has several restaurants and a large selection of good food. The food court is located on the side street adjacent to *Farmacia Similares*. *Farmacia Similares* is on a corner and across the street from the ADO bus terminal.

One block south and parallel to Avenida Tulum is Calle Sol. There more of the real Mexico is found.

The selection and variety of eating experiences is endless...take your unhurried time. This is the land of take it easy.

Tulum has an influx of Mexicans from the entire country and this amalgamation has brought with them their regional culinary specialties, which can be sampled all along the Riviera Maya.

El Camello: The place for seafood in Tulum.

For seafood, the fisherman's co-op restaurant and fresh fish market, *El Camello*, south of the downtown a couple of blocks, beats all for freshness and price.

Hotels, Hostels, and Beach Resorts

This area may be overbuilt in the accommodations department except at the absolute peak of the tourist season.

Beach resorts are in a wide range of categories, from the exclusive five-star all-inclusive where all you can eat and drink for one flat fee to backpacker camping.

One of the best water front camping places is Santa Fe, just south of the Mayan ruins. It is on the best beach.

For the economy minded traveler, hostels could be the best choice. In the last couple of years they seem to have sprouted up everywhere in the Tulum area. Still the best all around choice is the Tulum Bike Hostel (Hostel Lobo Inn) located at KM 230 on the main north-south highway close to the Tulum archeological ruins entrance road. For more information, email: bedbikeandbreakfastulum@hotmail.com

Dormitory beds start at ten dollars or $130 pesos and all lodgings include breakfast, bicycle use, pool, internet access, security lockers, purified drinking water, kitchen access, hot water showers, and more. Private rooms are available for two to twelve persons, and camping is also available. This is the perfect choice for eccentric peso pinchers.

Diving

Divers come to Tulum for the wide variety of diving experiences offered here. Diving guides are recommended that are certified for caves, *cenotes*, reefs and the sea. Scuba and snorkel trips make for unforgettable adventures you won't want to miss. Tulum has an abundance of dive shops, but the oldest and most reliable is Acuatic Tulum located on the main highway #307 by the stop light at the Cobá turn off and next to the 7-Eleven.

www.acuatictulum.com.mx/home_en.html
e-mail: alexalvareze@prodigy.net.mx

The lure of the Caribbean is enticing especially when you consider the clean air and clear water with temperatures that average 30°C or 86°F all year. There is a dry season that extends from November to May when precipitation is minimal, but what rain does fall is brief.

What are you waiting for?

16 - Muyil Ruins - A Side Trip from Tulum or Valladolid

Twenty-two kilometers south of Tulum is a remarkable link to Mayan ingenuity.

Muyil, also known as Chunyaxché, is located in a dense jungle setting. It is a Mayan inland seaport connected to the Caribbean Sea by lagoons and two man-made canals. It exists as a noteworthy testimonial to the engineering achievements of this remarkable Mayan civilization.

Muyil is a wonderful place to take a hike, mingle with tropical nature, and witness some unusual examples of the Mayan advanced infrastructure that still exist within this archeological zone.

This is a big place, so plan to do a lot of walking. To enjoy Muyil to its fullest, a half day of leisurely poking along will enhance your pleasurable experience immensely.

Entrance to Muyil.

After a short ride from the bus station in Tulum, the Mayab bus will let you off near the entrance. It is only a short walk to visit *El Castillo*, one of the tallest Mayan ruins on the east coast of the Caribbean.

In the late 1950s when this area was a territorial part of Mexico with literally no infrastructure, this place was only accessible by a five day jungle horseback ride from the end of the railroad line from Mérida or by coastal sailing vessel from the Caribbean island of Cozumel.

Pablo Bush Romero led one of the first expeditions to this "Lost City of the Maya." In his book, *Under the Waters of Mexico*, he wrote about his remarkable adventure: *After about thirty minutes of navigating through the channel, we entered the impressive lake of Chunyaxché, a marvel of archaeologists specializing in Mayan civilization. Precisely at the mouth of the channel, on the left side, we discovered the temple of Xlabpak... After crossing the lake, with its exquisitely blue water, we went through another canal. After several hours of navigating on the canal, we arrived at Lake Muyil, which was wide and not very deep. After landing on the dilapidated pier, we started our exploration by walking along a trail through the jungle, which ended in a clearing where there were two small huts inhabited by natives...*

Michel Peissel, explorer and author, visited Muyil in 1958. He wrote of his discovery of the Mayan city in his book, *Lost World of Quintana Roo: ...breaking through the treetops, the summit of the large pyramid I had noticed during my first visit to Chunyaxché. This was the mighty pyramid that the Mason-Spinden expedition had discovered in 1926 and that Charles Lindbergh had sighted from the air more than thirty years before our trip. I now learned from Coba-Cama that a few foreigners had come here since my first visit, arriving at the lagoon by way of the fishing camp of Boca de Paila... Chunyaxché was to surpass my wildest dreams. When, ten days later, we left Chunyaxché exhausted, we had uncovered no less than 108 mounds, temples, pyramids, and palaces...Chunyaxché to all appearances was the largest ancient Mayan city of Quintana Roo, the long-lost center of the Mayan coastal realm, the hub of the maritime civilization of the Mayas. Here was a city more formidable than Tulum, a city that extended for many miles around the tall pyramid that Lindbergh had seen.*

El Castillo, the pyramid spotted by Charles Lindbergh from the air.

On your jungle walk you will see the seventeen meter or nearly sixty foot tall partially restored Mayan temple that has the significance of being an observation platform and signaling station.

On the pinnacle of *El Castillo* is a platform that allows a view of the distant Caribbean Sea and all waterways linking it to Muyil. There is evidence that signal fires were built on its peak that may have been used to guide in the Mayan seafaring merchant vessels. Muyil began to populate by 300

B.C. This was centuries before such ancient Mayan cities as Chichén Itzá, Uxmal, and Tulum.

Explorer Pablo Bush Romero describes in his book *Under the Waters of Mexico* what he and his colleagues encountered at Muyil's *El Castillo*, a pyramid with steep steps and an oratory on top: *Under one of these steps we found a tunnel which led to another temple situated in the heart of the pyramid. According to Segovia, this temple was dedicated to the high priests. Along the passage were a series of niches. We put our hands deep into each niche to see if there were any archeological relics. When we reached the most important one in the center of the tunnel, Alfonso Arnold, by chance or though some kind of intuition, thought to turn his search light on first; He got such a scare that he recoiled almost as far as the front wall. Instead of archeological relics, what he saw there was a nest of deadly "nauyaca" or "sorda" or "four-nosed" snakes, the most poisonous in the Mexican paradise.*

It was a good thing that we frightened a few of these serpents because if anybody's hand had been bitten, it would have been necessary to resort to a primitive surgery technique of the chicleros. Since we carried no antidotes, this involved immediate amputation of the bitten limb with a machete without sterilization or anesthesia.

Built with a purpose, *El Castillo* is but one of nearly a hundred structures erected on these premises. Muyil was on one of many Mayan trading routes. Though some distance from the sea, the Maya excavated straight canals, one of five kilometers in length and the other one kilometer, cutting down into bedrock with nothing but hand tools to accomplish their enormous goal. This is a real seaport in the jungle.

Seagoing sailing freight canoes plied these waters.

The cumbersome sea salt from northern Yucatan could have only been transported by seagoing vessels. Other cargo items included cotton, cocao, copper, dyes, fish, honey, jade, and more.

The seagoing Maya utilized natural inlets and beaches along this coast, such as Tulum ruins, Tankah, Akumal, Xaac, Paamul, Chakalal, Xel-Ha and Xcaret. All of these landing ports had Maya temple ruins.

John on the boardwalk.

Leaving the area of *El Castillo* your next jaunt is through a canopy jungle on a boardwalk. This segment will take you about forty minutes. Take your time to sniff the flowers and admire the exotic jungle trees.

If you are tempted to venture off of the walkway, remember the venomous snakes. The pit viper *nauyaca* is found in this lowland habitat. Together with the rattlesnake, it is the chief cause of snakebite in the Yucatan Peninsula of Mexico.

Midpoint on your boardwalk trip is an observation tower. The observation tower offers a splendid view of the expansive surrounding jungle, lakes, lagoons, mangrove swamps, and the distant Caribbean, but climb at your own risk. The steps are steep and are for the young and adventurous.

Emerging from the jungle boardwalk you will find yourself at a lovely beach on Muyil Lagoon where guided tours are available. Several different excursions are offered including traversing the ancient Mayan canal system.

There is nothing like this anywhere. If nature is what you came to see, this is your place. Don't miss your opportunity.

The dock at Muyil lake.

Strolling back to the Muyil ruins from the lake, you will find yourself on an ancient Mayan *sacbe* road that has remnants of pre-Columbian ornate stone carvings along the way.

Pablo Bush Romero exclaims in his book *Under the Waters of Mexico*: *What amazing road engineers the Maya's were! I have traced from a helicopter one of those roads called "Sacbe" [white road] for over 100 kilometers. Undoubtedly, Tulum was the focal point of a coastal artery because every seven or eight kilometers there is a temple. The temples offered refuge to travelers, thus establishing centers of protection against cannibalistic Caribe Indians...*

The jungle diversity here is positively amazing. Your path around the Muyil Mayan ruins site gives you a look at the area's range of topography.

One of the temples at Muyil.

The jungle is literally full of temples in varying stages of restoration and degradation. Trees of considerable size have embedded themselves in the ancient structures.

If unchecked, the trees with their invasive root systems will pull them all down. It has been over five hundred years that the jungle has had a free hand to do its destruction here and yet these structures stubbornly stand.

For the return trip to Tulum, walk out to the main road, then to the bus stop a short distance south of the entrance to Muyil ruins and wave down a bus or van (*colectivo* taxi) for the short trip back to Tulum.

This side trip to Muyil is recommended to all those who truly want more than just another tourist trap.

Recommended reading related to Muyil:

The Lost World of Quintana Roo by Michel Peissel.
Under the Waters of Mexico by Pablo Bush Romero.
Final Report: An Archaelogists Excavates his Past by Michael D. Coe.
The Maya by Michael D. Coe.

17 - Ruins Explained

The Yucatan has a seemingly endless amount of ruins and relics of bygone years for travelers to explore.

A 1940s era stacked stone house.

Ruins Explained:

"What's the point in erecting more and more ruins?" he asked wistfully, looking round at his friends. Ruins of haciendas, ruins of churches, of schools—I had seen them everywhere; and the great ruins of the past, of Aztecs and Mayas. In fact, there was not a century that had not contributed its share from pre-conquest times to the present. Crumbling stones and adobe walls, the work of man destroyed by violence or neglect. We all sighed.

Excerpt from Magic Yucatan by Lilo Linke, 1950.

18 - Yucatan Roadways

The Yucatan roadways evolved over the centuries beginning with the Mayan *sacbe* infrastructure.

This glorious relic of Merida's wealthier and more prosperous years is the central railway station located on Calle 55 in the city center. Photo, 1985.

In the course of human events that shaped the cultural evolution of the Yucatan Peninsula, the *sacbe* road network erected by the ancient Maya laid the groundwork for transportation systems that continue in use to this very day.

Sacbe in the Mayan language literally means white road and was so named because of the fact that the Mayan road builders finished their *sacbe* road surfaces with a smooth plaster finish that was white. Using the fired heavily calcified *sahcab* earthen deposit found in Yucatan, it made relatively soft cement. Cement production required huge amounts of firewood, which accelerated the deforestation of the peninsula.

When the first *sacbe* roads were constructed remains a mystery. Before the arrival of the Spanish conquistadors, the

Mayan people built an extensive network of roads, which were remarkably straight and level. They did this without the use of any machinery.

Because the ancient Maya used no wheeled vehicles these *sacbe* road surfaces were very serviceable, but when the Spanish arrived and pressed these same roadways into service with horses and horse carts, they became rough and rocky.

This painting shows an early Yucatan passenger coach known as a *caricoché*, dating from the era before the age of rail, bouncing along a well worn rocky *sacbe* road.

John L. Stephens described the caricoché in his book *Incidents of Travel in Yucatan*:

The caricoché was drawn by three mules, and had in it a bed, on which we reclined at full length. At nine o'clock we entered the suburbs of Izamal, but fifteen leagues from Mérida. The streets had lamps, and were designated by visible objects, as at Mérida. Peeping through the curtain, we rode into the plaza, which was alive with people, dressed in clean clothes for the fiesta. There was an unusual proportion of gentlemen with black hats and canes, and some with military coats, bright and flashing to such a degree that we congratulated ourselves upon not having made our entry on horseback.

Until the advent of the Industrial Revolution and its huge demand for rope fiber, the Yucatan roads had not seen any upgrades for three centuries.

Machinery along with agriculture and a suitable climate coupled with hacienda mentality well practiced in the extrapolation of labor from the Maya were all the right ingredients for the explosive expansion of Yucatan's transportation system

This type of cart, called a *truk* was used in Yucatan on the early Decauville rails.

The first type of rail system to be used in Yucatan was called Decauville. Decauville was the name of a town in Belgium where the rail was imported from. The rail was fastened to steel ties and came in sections that only needed bolting together.

When henequen became a principal cash crop in Yucatan in the mid-1800s the demand quickly built to the point that a rail transport system became imperative. To move the product to market Decauville rails networked the peninsula connecting with the narrow gauge steam train system conveniently using some of the old Mayan *sacbe* roads. By the late 1800s more than 4,500 kilometers of this one- half meter wide track had been laid across the Yucatan Peninsula.

The above photo was taken in the 1980s in the main lobby of Cordamex, the state run henequen processing plant. The products Cordamex produced were on display: Rope, twine, fiber, mats, and woven yard goods were manufactured at this facility. Also in the photo is one of the mature henequen plants that this fiber is derived from.

Stockpiled henequen leaves or *pencas* at the Cordamex plant on the north side of Mérida are aboard the conveyer and ready to be processed.

With state of the art processing equipment Cordamex was in a good position to compete in the international marketplace. Synthetic manmade fibers were blamed for the collapse of this Yucatan industry, but mismanagement coupled with extravagantly high executive pay packages were rumored to have been a contributing factor.

Cordamex went from private to federal ownership and ultimately the State of Yucatan became the proprietor. Each change of hands seemed to see a larger and larger amount of wealthy benefactors bailing out until external and internal forces brought the peninsula's henequen business to near extinction.

Yucatan became the wealthiest state in Mexico driven by world demand for henequen fiber. It was produced here to such an extent that its total takeover of agriculture denuded the forests, displaced the *milpa* farmers, and actually altered the climatic conditions making northwestern Yucatan into a semiarid tropical environment. Ninety percent of the nearly one-thousand henequen haciendas were controlled by thirty families.

The above photo is of one of several of the original Baldwin steam locomotives manufactured in the U.S. that spent their long arduous lives fueled by *leña* or firewood and hauling freight and passengers from Mérida to Peto or Tizimín and all points in between. This narrow gauge railway system was still operational in the 1980s.

This engine is on display at the railway museum in Mérida, which is located on Calle 43 near the corner of Calle 50 in the city center.

The first steam train was to Progreso in 1881, Izamal 1890, Campeche 1904, Peto 1912, and Valladolid in 1913.

We made many memorable trips aboard the narrow gauge trains. A trip on the narrow gauge train was always a high point for friends that visited Yucatan.

There was no rail service to the Yucatan Peninsula from other parts of Mexico until 1950 and no paved roads connecting the rest of Mexico until 1960. Ship service linked Mérida to Veracruz, Havana, and the U.S. before roads and rail arrived in Yucatan.

Boarding the packed to capacity narrow gauge train to Peto with its 1890s vintage wooden coaches.

Waiting for the train.

The train's arrival was a major event all along the route attracting eager vendors and economy travelers.

Many of the passengers carried products to market in Mérida, which included live animals (turkeys, chickens, and pigs), and homegrown vegetables and fruits. They returned home with supplies that could only be purchased in Mérida.

Colorful vendors aboard the train sold native folk remedies and handcrafted trinkets. Entertainment was provided by singing guitarists who solicited tips.

Train schedule – October, 1984.

FERROCARRILES	NACIONALES DE	MEXICO
DIRECCION: Calle 55 x 48 y 50TELEFONOS:3 59 44	RECORIDOS	oct. 1984
	$150	$140
Mérida – Tizimin	Mérida – Valladolid	Mérida – Peto
Frecuencia: Diaria	Frecuencia: Diaria	Frecuencia:
Salida: 5:30 A.M.	Salida: 3:10 P.M.	Diaria
Llegada: 10:25 A.M.	Llegada: 8:00 P.M.	Salida: 2:00 P.M.
Tixkokob	Tixkokob	Llegada: 7:15
Euán	Euán	P.M.
Cacalchén	Cacalchén	Acanceh
Tekanto	Tekanto	Tecoh
Izamal	Izamal	Xcanchakan
Sitilpech	Sitilpech	Hunabchen
Hualactún	Hualactún	Ticul
Tunkas	Tunkas	Yotholin
Escape Cámara	Escape Cámara	Oxkutzcab
Quintana Roo	Quintana Roo	Akil
Dzitas	Dzitas	Tekax
Xuilub	Bolantún	Ticum
Espita	Tinum	Caxaytuk
Calotmul	Uayma	Tzucacab
Tizimín	Valladolid	Xoy
		Peto

This official train timetable for the narrow gauge train lists several scheduled stops where there wasn't a paved road to the landing, only a jungle path. We traveled to all of the above destinations on the narrow gauge and later the upgraded wide track train.

Narrow gauge diesel locomotive from the early 1980s.

Our friend Melchor Castro was the engineer on the Merida – Peto route of the narrow gauge train. He often invited us and our friends to ride along in the locomotive.

This is the rail station at Izamal on the line from Mérida to Tizimín in 1984.

At the Izamal railway station, this *calesa* was the only type taxi service at that time.

Izamal: Passengers and freight bound for the afternoon train to Mérida.

Three hundred and fifty pound bales of locally produced henequen arrive by horse cart to be loaded for transport to Mérida by train for processing.

After the Mérida train arrived in Tizimín and was unloaded, scavengers picked every last kernel of corn from the boxcars that were on the siding behind the terminal.

This old narrow gauge steam engine that proudly pulled the products that made Yucatan the richest state in Mexico around the time of the First World War now quietly rusts away on a rail siding in downtown Mérida unnoticed by speeding highway traffic.

Not all was lost from those glorious days of Yucatan's steam train travel. Back in the early 1970s Walt Disney came to Mérida and purchased the last serviceable narrow gauge steam locomotives and transported them to his new Florida amusement park.

John and Jane at Disney World with one of its painted and polished Baldwin locomotives that came from Yucatan.

Four of these engines were restored to a state of better than new, and two were used for replacement parts.

Pictured in this recent photo is a well-worn wooden cargo cart with tire treaded wheels, wooden saddle, and henequen harnesses. It will keep on pulling when this world runs out of gas.

19 - Buses and Colectivo Taxis

You haven't seen the real Yucatan until you bike and bus it.

The intention of this chapter is to assist those adventurers and bicyclers who wish to incorporate bus/taxi transport into their travel adventures in and out of Mérida, Valladolid, and Tulum.

First class and luxury buses will definitely get you there fast and efficiently, but for fun, excitement, and adventure, second class will take you to the places that tourists miss most. They travel to the out-of-the-way villages where you will meet the people that live there. Second class buses stop on demand, and take longer than first class buses, and they are much cheaper than first class.

The following information does not give a complete list of all the destinations that the numerous bus companies service. However, that current information can be found by visiting the websites given or calling the listed telephone numbers.

Not all buses have space for full-sized bicycles. Folding bicycles that are folded are best because they will go on or in all buses and *colectivo* taxis (vans), and even if there is no storage space below or luggage rack on top, many will accommodate your bicycle inside. You might have to buy an extra seat for the displaced space.

Full-sized bikes usually can be stowed below in the baggage compartment on first class buses and on the second class bus lines of Mayab and Orienté. There is sometimes a charge for a bicycle. On second class buses, the driver decides if you pay and on first class buses, the baggage handler will decide if there is an additional fee for a bicycle in the luggage compartment.

Buses and Bus Terminals of Valladolid

ADO bus terminal in Valladolid.

ADO bus terminal in Valladolid
Calle 39 on the corner with Calle 41
ADO, Mayab, and Orienté buses are at this terminal.

Centro bus terminal of Valladolid
Calle 37 and Calle 54
Centro has frequent bus service between Mérida and Cancún.
The route from Mérida travels the old highway through Izamal and Tunkás to Valladolid and then back roads to Cancún.

There are also *colectivo* taxis parked on the streets of Valladolid that will take you to most villages, to Tizimín, Mérida, and Cancún.

ADO bus terminal Tulum

The terminal is located towards the southern end of the main business district on Avenida Tulum.

You can purchase tickets and make connections to almost everywhere in Mexico from the Tulum ADO terminal. There is frequent service to Playa del Carmen and Cancun.

Colectivo taxis to Playa del Carmen depart across the street from the terminal.

Colectivo taxis to Felipe Carrillo Puerto and points south are parked on the street just south of the ADO terminal.

The terminal for colectivo taxis to Punta Allen is located on Avenida Tulum, on the same side of the street as ADO but about three blocks north.

Local taxis are parked in front of the terminal.

Cancún Bus Terminal
Calle Pino between Av. Uxmal and Av. Tulum
Destinations: Airport, Mérida, Valladolid, Tulum, Playa del Carmen, Bacalar, Chetumal, and Mexico City.

Buses from Cancún Airport
ADO has shuttle buses from the airport to downtown Cancún and to Playa del Carmen. The buses to downtown Cancún depart every thirty minutes from Terminal 3, and

then make a stop at Terminal 2. There are ticket offices near the exits at both terminals.

Buses and Bus Terminals of Mérida, Yucatan

CAME bus terminal - Centro de autobuses Mérida
Calle 70 between Calle 69 and 71
Downtown Mérida
Tel. 999-924-8391, 923-4440, 923-4443
Lines: ADO, ADO-GL and Platino
www.ado.com.mx

CAME bus terminal - *Centro de autobuses Mérida.*

The Platino buses are fabulous; they have extra wide fully reclining luxury seats, his and hers rest rooms, and a wet bar with coffee, tea, bottled water, and soft drinks included. A kit containing ear plugs, ear phones, eye covers, plus a pillow and blanket are standard equipment. Many people ride these buses though the night and save the price of a hotel room.

Destinations from CAME: Cancún, Campeche, Ciudad Del Carmen, Cordoba, Playa del Carmen, Chetumal, Tulum, Veracruz, Minatitlán, E. Zapata, Palenque, Puebla, México City, Valladolid, Ocosingo, Tuxtla-Gtz, Chichén Itzá, San Cristobal de las Casas, and Belize City, Belize.

ADO operates most of the first class buses, which include Platino and GL. They have the best quality and set the standard for all Mexican buses. You will always see these buses professionally driven, and in good condition.

Mérida Fiesta Americana

Across Calle 60 from the Hotel Fiesta Americana in Plaza Bonita
Calle 60 and Av. Colón
Tel. 999-925-0910
Lines: ADO-GL, Platino plus Cancún Airport van
Destinations: Cancún, Cancún Airport, and Villahermosa.

Mérida Alta Brisas

Alta Brisas Mall
Avenida Racho Correa
Near Star Medica
Lines: ADO-GL, Platino plus Cancún Airport van
Destinations: Cancún, Cancún Airport.

TAME – Terminal de Autobuses Mérida
Calle 69 between Calles 68 and 70
Downtown

TAME bus terminal - Terminal de Autobuses Mérida.

This is where you will find what is called the economical buses, plus the first class bus to Chetumal, Clase Europea. It leaves from this terminal at 10 a.m., 4 p.m, 10:30 p.m., and midnight. The trip takes 5 ½ hours.   The Clase Europea bus has toilets, but most of the buses leaving from this terminal do not.

TAME is also where you will find; OCC, Mayab, ATS, Oriente, and TRT bus lines.   This is where you find the Mayab buses that go to Ticul, Oxkutzcab, and Tekax.

Buses from here run to the Caribbean coast, all over Yucatan, Campeche, and Tabasco. Here you find the buses to Uxmal and Holbox. Also, you can buy tickets here for all the ADO buses, although they leave from the CAME terminal, which is around the corner on Calle 70.

Terminal Autobuses del Noreste, Oriente and Lus
Calle 67 between Calle 50 and 52
Near the corner with Calle 50
Tel. 999 924 6355 and 923 0548

Terminal Autobuses del Noreste, Oriente and Lus.

These buses are all second class, meaning that they have no on-board toilet facilities, and stop anywhere on demand.

This is the best terminal to use for day trips that will take you off the main roads to villages and old haciendas. Buses from this station run to the Mayan ruins of Mayapán. If you buy a ticket to Mayapán, make sure you specify the ruins of Mayapán (*ruinas de Mayapán or zona archeologica de Mayapán*) or you may end up in the village of Mayapán many kilometers from the archeological site.

Folding bicycles are no charge, but, they have a tight fit in the small luggage compartments under these buses.

The Autobuses del Noreste ticket counter also sells ADO tickets to all destinations in Mexico.

Three bus lines are here, Noreste, Orienté and Lus. Destinations from Mérida on Noreste line and Oriente are Motul, Izamal, Espita, Dzidzantún, Dzilám González, Dzilám de Bravo, Buctzotz, Tizimín, Rio Lagartos, San Felipe, Kantunikin, Valladolid, and Cancún, and more.

From Mérida on the Lus line; Acanceh, Tecoh, Teabo, Chumayel, Tekit, Mamá, Maní, Oxkutzcab, Peto, Cuzamá, Homún and Huhí, and more.

Terminal del Centro - Centro Autobuses

Calle 65 between 46 and 48 next to *Casa del Pueblo* in downtown Mérida. Tel. 923 9962, 923 9941 extension 15 Destinations from Mérida on Centro Autobuses: These buses head towards Valladolid and Cancún with many stops along the way,

including Tixkokob, and Izamal. Centro also has buses to Motul. These buses make frequent stops. They have no onboard toilet facilities.

Autoprogreso - Progreso Bus Terminal
Calle 62 No. 524 between Calle 65 and 67
Downtown Mérida   Tel. 999-928-3965

Autoprogreso - Progreso Bus Terminal.

Autoprogreso has comfortable, airconditioned buses that depart for Progreso about every 20 minutes between 5 a.m. and 10:30 p.m. from their terminal in Mérida on Calle 62 located between Calle 65 and 67. Buses out of this station also serve the beach towns of Chuburná Puerto and Chelém.

Vans - *Colectivo taxis* or *Combis* from Mérida

These fast moving multi-passenger vans park on the street or have terminals at numerous designated spots in downtown Mérida, near and around the main municipal market and also in the Parque San Juan located between Calle 62 and Calle 64 and Calle 69a in downtown Mérida.

There are *colectivo* taxis to almost all villages in Yucatan.

Most *colectivo* taxis take departure when they have sufficient passengers.

The nice thing about these *colectivo* taxis is that you can flag them down anywhere, and they are numerous throughout Yucatan. So, returning to Mérida is quick and easy. We often times bus out to our biking area, and then we return by *colectivo* taxi, which will get you back to Mérida fast.

Taxi terminal for Tekax located on Calle 62 near Calle 69a, Parque San Juan in downtown Mérida.

Numerous *colectivo* taxis park near the main market on Calle 67 near the corner of Calle 54. The first one is from Mérida to Acanceh and Tecoh.

The vans will stop anywhere, but full sized bicycles could be a problem unless you find a taxi with a roof-top rack, and in that case the sky is the limit. Expect to pay an extra fare for your bike if it is loaded top-side. Almost all of these taxis have room for a couple of folding bicycles inside behind the rear seats. They rarely charge extra for the folding bikes.

The possibility of end destinations with these *colectivo* taxis is extensive.

You haven't seen the real Yucatan until you bike and bus it.

After more than a quarter century of doing these excursions, we still have a long list of end-destinations to explore.

What are you waiting for? Come on and have the adventure of a lifetime.

It is curious that with the advent of the automobile and the airplane, the bicycle is still with us. Perhaps people like the world they can see from a bike, or the air they breathe when they're out on a bike... Or because they like the feeling of being able to hurtle through air one minute, and saunter through a park the next, without leaving behind clouds of choking exhaust, without leaving behind so much as a footstep. ~Gurdon S. Leete

Excerpted from *The Quotable Cyclist: Great Moments of Bicycling Wisdom, Inspiration and Humor* by Bill Strickland.

Map

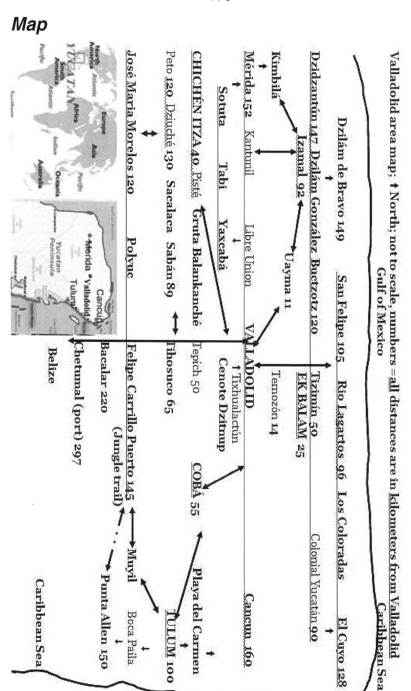

Valladolid area map; ↑ North; not to scale, numbers = all distances are in kilometers from Valladolid

Gulf of Mexico

Caribbean Sea

Dzilám de Bravo 149

Dzidzantún 147 Dzilám González Buctzotz 120

Mérida 152   Kantunil   Libre Union

Kimbilá

Izamal 92   Uayma 11

Sotuta   Tabi   Yaxcabá

CHICHÉN ITZA 40 Pisté   Gruta Balankanché

Peto 120 Dziuché 130   Sacalaca Sabán 89

José María Morelos 120   Polyuc

San Felipe 105   Rio Lagartos 96   Los Coloradas   El Cuyo 128

Tizimín 50

EK BALAM 25

Temozón 14   Colonial Yucatán 90

VALLADOLID

↑ Tixhualactún
Cenote Dzitnup

Tepich 50

Tihosuco 65   COBÁ 55   Cancún 160

Felipe Carrillo Puerto 145

(Jungle trail)   Muyil   Playa del Carmen

Bacalar 220   TULUM 100

Chetumal (port) 297   Punta Allen 150   Boca Paila

Belize

Caribbean Sea

Bilingual Glossary of Terms

Mayan = (m) Spanish = (sp)

Agua oxigenada (sp) hydrogen peroxide.

Auto de Fe (sp) In 1478 King Ferdinand and Queen Isabella had received permission from Pope Sixtus IV to name Inquisitors throughout their domain to protect Catholicism as the true faith. They immediately began establishing permanent trials and developing bureaucracies to carry out investigations. Franciscan missionaries brought the Inquisition to the Yucatan. A major aspect of the tribunals was the *auto de fe* religious ceremony. In July 1562, Friar Diego de Landa held an *auto de fe* Inquisitional ceremony in Maní, burning a number of Maya books and 5000 idols, saying that they were "works of the devil." This act and numerous incidents of torture at the monastery were used to speed the mass adoption of Catholicism throughout the region.

Cal (sp) Hydrated lime.

Calabasa, (sp) Name to several varieties of squash grown and harvested for their seeds. The seeds are used in a wide variety of ways in Mayan cooking.

Calesa (sp) Open horse drawn carriage used for taxi or touring.

Callejeros (sp) Street dogs.

Campesino (sp) Country man.

Can sacbe (m) Mayan word meaning road of snakes.

Carnival A week long pre-lent/Easter festival of parades, street dancing, noise making and beer drinking with roots in a prehistoric pagan spring celebration. Mérida has the second largest event in Mexico. The world's largest carnival is in Brazil with New Orleans being the largest in the United States. (carnaval = Spanish/ English = carnival)

Carretera (sp) A major highway or road.

Caste War, guerra de las castas (sp) A protracted battle between the Yucatec Maya and Spanish colonialists of Yucatan known as the *guerra de las castas*. Begun in 1847, this conflict ultimately divided the Yucatan peninsula into Campeche state, Yucatan state and the Territory of Quintana Roo.

Caste War Route. The road to visiting the towns and places affected in the Caste War.

Cenotes (sp) Derived from the Mayan Dzonot. In Yucatan a *cenote* is a sinkhole formed in the rock strata that exposes water to the surface. **Zona de Cenotes** (sp) Area with numerous sinkholes.

Cerros, (sp) In Yucatan, over grown Mayan ruin mounds are referred to as *cerros* or hills.

Chaltune (m) Mayan cistern for the collection of rain water.

Chan Santa Cruz Indians. They were also known as the **Cruzob** Maya. These were separatist Maya of the Caste War era who established their own territory, religion and capital city in the isolated jungle. Their capital in the jungle, Chan Santa Cruz, was the site of a Mayan temple named Balam-Nah, or House of the Jaguar Priest. It was built using labor of captive white prisoners of the Caste War. Chan Santa Cruz was overrun by Mexican federal troops in 1901, and occupied until the Mexicans capitulated in 1915, marking the longest Indian insurgency in the Americas.

Chiclero (sp) a gatherer of chicle. Chicle is a gum from the latex of the sapodilla tree (zapote) used as the chief ingredient of chewing gum.

Chilam Balam of Chumayel. The so-called books of Chilam Balam are handwritten in the Yucatec language using the Latin alphabet. They are named after the towns where they were originally kept. The book of the Chilam Balam of Chumayel is a late 18th-century manuscript copy of a Yucatec Maya chronicle, written and illustrated in Chumayel, Yucatan. The text chronicles the Spanish conquest of the Yucatan, and provides information about the prophecy of

Chilam Balam, the calendar, astronomy, creation of the world, rituals, and other subjects.

Ciclopista (sp) Bicycle path.

Ciénega (sp) Coastal lagoons.

Cocal (sp) A coconut plantation. Men who worked on a cocal were called cocaleros.

Cochinita pibil (sp) A traditional Mayan slow roasted pork dish. Often a whole pig is roasted in a rock-lined pit. The pork is marinated in sour orange juice and wrapped in banana leaves for cooking.

Cocina económica (sp) An inexpensive restaurant usually run by one or two women. It is sometimes located in their home. It is open for the midday meal. Two or three different Yucatecan dishes are offered each day. All meals come with tortillas and usually soup or rice, and are always accompanied by the Yucatecan sizzling habanero chili sauce. You can order a full portion or half a portion. Take out is almost always available.

Codice (sp) Old manuscript dealing with noteworthy points of antiquity.

Colectivo taxi (sp) In Yucatan these are vans that circulate like buses. They travel fast and will stop anywhere to pick up passengers, if they have room.

Colonial. In Yucatan, colonial can refer to the type of building construction; Spanish or French, or it can refer to a town or village established at the time when Mexico was a colony of Spain.

Comal (sp) Name of cooking utensil made of tin or pottery used over a wood fire. It is painted white with *cal* or hydrated lime to keep the food from sticking. It is principally used for making tortillas.

Copal (sp) Pitchy resinous wood burned in Mayan ceremonies to yield a distinctive aroma.

Corbel (sp) Name given to a type of arch used in ancient Mayan construction. It is not a true arch.

Cult of the Talking Cross. During the Caste War many Maya rejected the faith of the conquistadors, and established their own religion that was an amalgamation of the ancient Mayan and Catholicism. An off shoot of this cult religion is active to this day and is referred to as the *cult de la Santisimo Cruz*.

Curadura (sp) Medicine man or woman.

Dia de los Muertos (sp) Day of the Dead, a Mexican national holiday with area variations. A holiday festival observed with religious connotations and subdued partying that is not morbid. Graves are visited, decorated, and picnicking is done with a traditional chicken stuffed cornbread called *pan de muerto* or bread of the dead. In Yucatan the event is held October 30- 31, and November 1-2, and Mayan tradition is commingled with Spanish custom. It is common to see special decorated altars with ceremonial events in area restaurants and private homes across Yucatan. Brightly colored little sugar skull candies are traditional.

Dicho (sp) A saying. For example; *pueblo chico, inferno grande* or small town, big hell.

Domicilio conocido (sp) Address is known. In small communities where the houses are not numbered and/or have no names for the streets, a person's mailing or delivery address would be their name plus *domicilio conocido*.

Dorado (sp) Golden.

El Laberinto (sp) The labyrinth.

El Pensamiento (sp) The Thinker.

Encomienda (sp) Land awarded as payment to Spanish mercenaries: a system that was employed by the Spanish crown during the colonization of the Americas. In the *encomienda*, the Spanish crown granted a person a specified number of natives for whom they were to take responsibility. In theory, the receiver of the grant was to protect the natives from warring tribes, and to instruct them in the Spanish language, and in the Catholic faith: in return they could extract tribute from the natives in the form of labor, gold or other products. In practice, the difference between *encomienda* and slavery could be minimal. Natives were forced to do strenuous labor and subjected to extreme punishment and death if they resisted.

Folkloric dances. The traditional dance and music of Yucatan is the Jarana. The Jarana dates back at least two centuries and is strongly influenced by the indigenous Maya culture. The traditional dress of the Yucatecan Jarana is the *terno*, a huipil made of white cotton and decorated with colorful embroidered flowers. The simple dress of the male Jarana dancer is the white *guayabera* or *filipino* shirt, white pants, a red handkerchief hung from the belt, a Panama hat, and a pair of white sandals, known as *caclis*.

Frijol con puerco (sp) A meal made with black beans and pork traditionally eaten on a Monday in Yucatan. Do not confuse this with any canned products from north of the border. This is a gourmet delight.

Guayaberas (sp) Traditional Yucatecan dress shirt.

Grutas (sp) Caves

Habanero (sp) Extremely hot chili pepper common in Yucatan, not believed to be indigenous. In the markets, the ladies selling these peppers cover their hands with a plastic bag when handling them.

Haciendas (sp) In Yucatan, a large landed estate. The hacienda originated in the Spanish colonial period and survived into the 20th century. The Maya were theoretically free wage earners on haciendas, but in practice their employers were able to bind them to the land, primarily by keeping them in a state of perpetual indebtedness. By the 19th century, as much as half of Mexico's rural population was entangled in the peonage system. Many haciendas were broken up by the Mexican Revolution.

Hamaca (sp) Hammock. The majority of people in Yucatan sleep in hammocks. Hammocks were developed and employed in the Americas before the arrival of the Spanish conquistadors, and continue to be made and used widely throughout Yucatan to this day. The most comfortable Yucatecan hammocks use nylon strings for their end sections but cotton for the main body.

Horchata (sp) A sweetened rice drink served cold or over ice.

Huevos a la Mexicana (sp) Huevos a la Mexicana are scrambled eggs cooked with chopped *serrano* chilies, onions, and tomatoes. They are served with refried beans and hot tortillas.

Huevos Motuleños (sp) A savory Yucatecan breakfast creation is built of toasted tortillas covered with refried black beans, fried eggs, tangy tomato sauce, green peas, chopped ham and grated fresh cheese accompanied by French bread to soak up the sauce and golden fried bananas. This dish originated in the town of Motul, thus motuleños meaning from Motul.

Huevos rancheros (sp) A classic Mexican breakfast, huevos rancheros are fried eggs served upon lightly fried hot corn tortillas and smothered in a tomato-chili sauce. They are often served with refried beans and slices of avocado.

Huinic (m) **El Huinic.** He is a typical Mayan field worker who has tended the farmlands of Yucatan for countless centuries. A day's ration of water is carried in the gourd at his waist and a bag containing his pozol, cooked corn dough. He will mix the pozol with water and some chili peppers for his day's sustenance. The traditional garb consists of a small brim straw hat, white shirt, trousers rolled up to his knees, simple flat sandals of henequen twine, cloth pouch and water gourd hung from his waist. His universal cutting tool shaped like a hook is called a *coá*.

Huipil also spelled **hipil (sp)** A white smock type dress richly adorned with embroidery and worn over a lace trimmed slip. It is the traditional dress of indigenous Mayan women.

Jamaica (sp) Hibiscus tea.

Jefe (sp) Boss.

Jipi (sp) Local name given by the people of Becal, Campeche, to the palm and the palm fibers which are woven to make Panama hats.

Kilómetro (sp) Kilometer. A kilometer is 1000 meters or .62 statue miles.

Lavabo mano (sp) Hand washing sink.

Legua (sp) A league (*legua*) is officially three miles or 4.8 kilometers. Here in Yucatan there is no official equivalent. The Maya reckon one league to be the distance a person can walk in one hour, and that will depend upon whether this is on a good flat road or through awful terrain.

Leña (sp) Wood cut for cooking fires.

Maiz (sp) Corn.

Masa (sp) Corn that has been boiled with lime and then ground into dough.

Maseca (sp) Dried masa to which water is added to make corn dough for tortillas.

Metate (sp) A carved flat stone used by the ancient Maya to grind corn using a *mano,* a round cylinder shaped stone rolled over the corn that was placed on the surface of the *metate.*

Mayab (m) Yucatan.

Mestiza (sp) In Yucatan, a county woman who dresses in a huipil is called a *mestiza.*

Mestizo (sp) In Mexico, a person of mixed cultural heritage.

Milpa (sp) A cornfield or plot of land worked by an indigenous farmer.

Molcajete (sp) A stone mortar and pestle used for grinding chilies, spices and herbs.

Molino (sp) A place where corn is taken to be ground by a machine.

Mosquitero (sp) A mosquito net used to cover a bed or hammock.

Nixtamal, **nixtamalizado**. (sp) Nixtamalization is the process of cooking corn with lime, which provides for the release of niacin into the diet. Beans, when consumed with corn that has been *nixtamalizado* provides the amino acids required to balance the diet for protein.

Nopal (sp) Prickly pear cactus. The young tender leaves are used in the cuisine of Mexico.

Palapa (sp) Mayan thatched roof home.

Paletas (sp) Popsicles made of fresh fruits and juices.

Panaderia (sp) Bakery.

Panuchos (sp) **Buut 'bil bu'ul waaj** (m) A fried fresh tortilla stuffed with black beans and topped with shredded chicken or turkey and lettuce.

Periférico (sp) A big city peripheral road.

Pescadores (sp) Fishermen

Plaza grande (sp) A public square, main plaza or park, also referred to as the *zócalo*.

Plaza de Toros (bull ring) Major cities in Spain and Latin America have amphitheater sized bull rings known as *Plaza de Toros* where scheduled bullfights, usually six in a series, pit a swordsmen against a bull; many area variations exist. Small villages erect wooden scaffolding amphitheaters for seasonal festivals around Mexico.

Poc chuc (m) Thinly sliced pork marinated in the juice of sour orange and grilled over charcoal. It is served with a red onion relish, tomato sauce, black bean soup, comatose level hot habanero sauce, and fresh hand made tortillas.

Pool kan-es also spelled **polkanes** (m) deep fried cakes of masa (corn dough) filled with *ibes*, a white lima bean, toasted ground squash seeds and chives.

Potaje de Lenteja (sp) This is a lentil stew with a variety of meats and vegetables.

Pozol (sp) Pozol is made by fermenting corn dough, which is rolled into balls. The drink is made by soaking the dough in water and adding chili, honey or sugar. In some places, chocolate is added.

Puchero (sp) A meat and vegetable stew traditionally served on Sunday in Yucatan.

Retablo (sp) An altarpiece of carved and painted wood that is usually gilded and displays religious paintings, relief carvings, and sculpted figures.

Sacbe (m) Sacbeob (plural of sacbe) Smooth, straight and nearly level white surfaced and plastered raised pedestrian roadways linking important Mayan sites. Not to be confused with "camino blanco" a limestone gravel surfaced road usually of Spanish origins.

Salbute (sp) A fresh tortilla fried in lard or oil until puffed and golden, then topped with layers of shredded chicken or turkey, lettuce or cabbage, red pickled onion, and topped with a sliced tomato.

Si Kil Pac (m) This is a flavorful nutritious Mayan dish of dried ground squash seeds mixed with diced tomatoes, habanero chili, onions, sour orange, and cilantro. It is served cold, and eaten with tortillas chips.

Suero (sp) A drink or powder used to replace bodily electrolytes. It is available at all pharmacies in Mexico.

Taller de Bordado (sp) A factory or workshop where embroidered clothing are made.

Telenovela (sp) Name given to a type of serial dramatic television program popular in Mexico.

Toh (m) Name for the mot-mot bird. In Spanish it is *pájaro relojero*. This bird has a long pendulum type tail.

Topes (sp) Speed bumps used to slow road traffic. In Mexico they take many different forms. On coastal roads large ropes are used as *topes*.

Tortillaria (sp) A shop that sells fresh hot tortillas. In Yucatan they are of corn and produced by machine.

Triciclo (sp) In Yucatan it is a cargo cart coupled to a pusher bicycle that may be adapted to a variety of uses, the most common in villages being a tricycle taxi (*tricitaxi*).

Truk (sp) In Yucatan, a *truk* is a type of cart mounted on Decauville rails and pulled by a horse. It was used in the henequen fields to haul the henequen leaves to the processing plant, and also to a carry the baled product to a nearby port for shipping.

Tunkul (m) Ceremonial log drum.

Vigas (sp) Ceiling beams made of wood in colonial times and today are made of pre-stressed cement beams.

Ya mero... **no tarda mucho**...**falta poco**! (sp) Almost there, not much longer, only lacking a little.

Yucatec Maya referring to the Mayan language spoken on the Yucatan Peninsula, distinctly different than that of Guatemala or Chiapas.

Zapote aka **sapote** (sp) Sapodilla is a fruit native to southern Mexico. The sap from the *zapote* tree is harvested for its high latex content and is called *chicle* and used in making chewing gum. The wood of the zapote tree is deep brown in color, very dense and hard. It is durable with exceptional resistance to decay. The ancient Maya used it in place of stone for headers in the doorways of their temples.

Zapotitos (sp) A candy made with ground pumpkin seeds.

Zócalo (sp) A public square, main plaza or park, also referred to as the *plaza grande*.

Select Bibliography

This is a list of books that inspired us in our travels and exploration of the Yucatan and led us to the places that tourists miss most.

Ambivalent Conquests by Inga Clendinnen
Here and There in Yucatan by Alice Dixon
Identifying Villa Carlota: German Settlements in Yucatan, México, During the Second Empire (1864-1867) by Alma Judith Durán-Merk
Incidents of Travel in Yucatan by John L. Stephens
Life in Mexico by Madame (Frances Erskine Inglis) Calderón de la Barca, 1843
Mayan Missions by Richard and Rosalind Perry
Magic Yucatan by Lilo Linke
Six Months in Mexico by Nellie Bly, 1888
The American Egypt: A Record of Travel in Yucatan by Channing Arnold and Frederick J. Tabor Frost
The Caste War of Yucatan by Nelson A. Reed
The Cult of the Holy Cross by Charlotte Zimmerman
The Final Report by Michael Coe
The Folk-Lore of Yucatan by Daniel G. Brinton
The Maya Indians of Southern Yucatan and Northern British Honduras by Thomas Gann, 1908
The Maya by Michael Coe
The Lost World of Quintana Roo by Michel Peissel 1958
The True History of Chocolate by Sophie and Michael Coe
Time Among The Maya by Ronald Wright
Under the Waters of Mexico by Pablo Bush Romero
Yucatan: A World Apart by Edward H. Mosley and Edward D. Terry
A Yucatan Kitchen by Loretta Miller
Yucatan's Magic – Mérida Side Trips: Treasures of Mayab by John M. Grimsrud

Yucatan is the place to relax; you don't have to rush here. Take the time to enjoy a good book, not just read it.

Useful Information

Yucatan Today: Free monthly tourist guide magazine with excellent maps and tourist related information. It is available at hotels, restaurants, and information centers in Yucatan. Consult their website for the up-to-date information on festivals and events in Yucatan: http://yucatantoday.com

Bicycle tours

Bike Mexico with Basil and Alix; exceptional Yucatan tours + western México. www.bikemexico.com

MexiGo in downtown Valladolid offers guided bicycle day tours + bike rentals   http://mexigotours.com

Helpful websites

The author's websites and blogs:

www.bicycleyucatan.com

http://bingsbuzz.blogspot.com

www.bicycleyucatan.blogspot.com

www.yucatanfortravelers.wordpress.com

About the Author

John M. Grimsrud lives with his wife Jane in Mérida, Yucatan, in an ecologically friendly home of his own design. He has been biking, photographing, exploring, and writing about the Yucatan for over twenty-five years.

Prior to seeking a new life of adventure in Yucatan, Mexico, John and his wife lived aboard their home built 46-foot sailboat *Dursmirg* for many years.

John has published *Travels of Dursmirg*, a four book series about his life aboard *Dursmirg*. John is author of *Yucatan's Magic-Mérida Side Trips*, the first book in his *Yucatan for Travelers* series.

His books are available in paperback and digital editions online and through most booksellers throughout the world.

About our Books

The *Travel of Dursmirg* series ©2012 by John M. Grimsrud is in four volumes: *Sailing Beyond Lake Superior*, *Sailing the Sea Islands*, *Sailing the Florida Keys*, and *Sailing to St. Augustine.*

The first three volumes were previously published in 2010. They have been renamed, updated, upgraded, and reformatted.

Sailing Beyond Lake Superior, *Travels of Dursmirg*, Vol. 1

This adventure story began as an idea and unfolded into a dream come true.

An obsession of escape materialized in 1972 with the building and launching of the dreamboat, *Dursmirg*. The motivations and inspirations for the five year plan were hastened by the revelation that youth only comes to you one time.

John and Jane went over the horizon and out to sea on their adventurous voyage.

From Duluth-Superior, they crossed the Great Lakes to New York City. Snow turned them south. It was an enchanting journey, and in more than one place they felt tempted to stay. But there was always the thought of Florida driving them on.

They arrived in fairyland. Destiny planted them in St. Augustine.

The first winter in Florida's waters they met incredible characters and mingled with the natives who made them appear like archconservatives.

This story relates the exciting happenings and action-packed personalities that forever altered their lives and changed its course.

This true love story that began with desires and aspirations then molded into reality was a stepping stone and spring board for the adventuresome life that took them to totally new dimensions. This is the first of four volumes in a series.

Sailing the Sea Islands, *Travels of Dursmirg*, Volume 2

Gone fishin' instead of just a wishin'

On Thanksgiving Day, 1972, they anchored at Daufuskie Island, South Carolina, their first taste of this enchanted land. They were impressed with the beautiful islands that tempted them to stay, but Florida was beckoning. They pressed on south through Georgia to Florida, which was the culmination of a five year plan.

On May 22, 1973, after spending a glorious winter in St. Augustine, Florida, they pulled their anchor and headed north.

Now they would be returning with the time to enjoy life to the fullest. This wonderful new world that awaited them was filled with dazzling surprises.

Sailing the Sea Islands is about pristine beaches, secluded anchorages, fun loving people, fishing adventures, and seafood experiences spiced with delectable southern cooking.

Jane and John had been neophytes when it came to salt water fishing; they had a lot to learn and would discover the local tricks for living out of the sea.

These experiences turned out to be among the very finest of their lives, especially when they became acquainted with the clever secrets and culinary delights of Southern cooking.

In this volume Jane has added her all-time best *Recipes from the Galley of Dursmirg*, featuring Southern cooking focused on Sea Island seafood using native ingredients.

Sailing the Florida Keys, *Travels of Dursmirg*, Volume 3

"We are going where the wind blows, when the spirit moves us, and the price is right." These were the driving forces that would be fulfilled beyond their wildest expectations.

Using St. Augustine, Florida, as a home base, winter sailing sojourns south always included the Indian River where lifelong friendships were cemented, bountiful seafood harvested, and anchorages were a slice of paradise.

Biscayne Bay was a cruising sail boater's dream come true with bountiful seafood, neat anchorages, and magical Miami there when your desires were tempted.

Dinner Key, Coconut Grove and Miami were all pulsating with an endless array or interesting things to do. Marvelous Cuban restaurants, back to the earth sun seekers, and salty sailors all added to the flavor.

Sailing the Florida Keys proved to be the best sailing, fishing, and exploring to be found anywhere. They saw the Keys that nearly nobody got to see; under its waters and away from highways. West of Key West only boaters ventured... a Utopian paradise for a privileged few.

Sailing to St. Augustine: *Travels of Dursmirg*, Volume 4

In Sailing to St. Augustine you will meet a mix of characters that are entertaining, amusing, and witty, and learn about the history of St. Augustine from the author's perspective in his search for the Fountain of Youth. John and Jane designed and built their dreamboat, sailed away, and lived with nature, out of the sea and off the land for fifteen glorious years— mission accomplished. Their dream came true.

In this final book of the *Travels of Dursmirg* series, *Sailing to St. Augustine*, they step into the world of St. Augustine and meet the people, some of them rogues and social misfits, who made their time in St. Augustine a one-of-a-kind experience.

They would discover the story of the Fountain of Youth and the intriguing history of St. Augustine. Discover how St. Augustine, as a home base, perpetuated their adventures into even more far flung new frontiers.

This story relates the action-packed events and exciting personalities that forever altered their lives and changed its course in St. Augustine, a place caught in the cross-hairs of time.

Looking for a New Frontier: *The Story of the Edwin Pearson Family*, by Jane A. Pearson Grimsrud

This is a true people story. Not just an adventure story. Not just an immigration story. This is a story of the people that made America great.

The story starts in Skåne, Sweden, where Edwin's father's dream of America began.

Chronicled here are the dreams, desires, aspirations and drives that motivated the Pearson family to make the cut-over land of Northern Wisconsin their home.

This narrative is related with intriguing anecdotes and spiced with Old Country humor. You will find a reflection of grass roots home spun Americana in every one of the real people who laid the foundation of a community that was part of the American dream.

Yucatán's Magic-Mérida Side Trips: Treasures of Mayab by John M. Grimsrud is now part of the **Yucatan for Travelers** series.

In *Yucatan's Magic-Mérida Side Trips* you will find the author's favorite travel adventure trips of the places, excursions and outings which he likes for different reasons. Among them; tranquility, history, a view of picturesque villages, a connection with the ancient Maya, changing landscape, and a look at another aspect of life, which will take you out of the mainstream and off the beaten path.

There is nothing to be gained by hurrying and worrying through the only lifetime you have got in this world. So, get out of life's rut and busy trap and find a new frontier and celebrate life here in the land of the Maya.

Yucatan's magic still abounds and is yours to discover off the main roads, away from tourist traps and trinket shops.

With unstructured time your destination will be free of emptiness and idleness.

Slow down your pace and take note of what is around you. *Yucatan's Magic - Mérida Side Trips* is your key to an adventure of a lifetime.

Acknowledgements

Special thanks to Ryan and Dominique Barras for sharing with us their incredible wedding story and photos.

Judy and Richard Lundeen have helped us in all of our published works. They have pitched in and done whatever was asked of them. Their talents are many.

We are grateful...a special thank you to Judy and Dick.

Index

Made in the USA
San Bernardino, CA
29 December 2015